...It exists...

00i00

Published by *FourReal* Publishers

An international platform producing works of interest

Produced together from the efficacious residual effects

of the

International Peace Collective Collaboration

A community of people who choose to write under pseudonyms
leaving you to enjoy the work without the influence of anything
other than the effort they have made on your life.

00i00

A society of peace unfolding before your eyes...

'Family Matters'

ISBN: 978-0-244-26074-3

1st Edition

Year of Creation 2019

Date of Publishing: 08/2/2020

THE INSPIRATIONAL MEDIATIONS PRAYERS AND
INSPIRED THOUGHTS

FROM THE LOVE OF EIRE (LAND)

THE PLACE THAT RAISED ME IN THE

LOVE OF SAINTS, SCHOLARS AND SAVIOURS

By

Mag R Westlife

Contents

~~~

How to Use This Book

As you progress the chapters of this book write the page numbers in the contents page...

Why? (answer that here)

Raw errors and type errors...

are four you...

This text is deliberately incorrect because it is for learning from in mind and heart. This gives a great deal of provocation to many sides of you and the world. For the students who have been writing this alongside the author and growing with it represents the material fact that it was and is possible...

Do correct errors as you find them or improve them. Therefore lessons will continue using this text and you can use it to roll out any lessons we may have shared and adapt them for yourselves.

Welcome...

Welcome to the short book promised to the 'Good People of Ireland' who have become close family and friends. Traditions and values foundered on morals and a confident attitude in presenting oneself for all one is. A shameless regard to express oneself and ones views in a way free from prejudice and to attentive ears who well understood that in all dialogue there is value to be added to both views of a conversation and therefore, lives.

The acceptance of others here and the celebration of the common differences are refreshing. I fell in love with the Irish nation and here is where my heart will reside, ever a place of mutual kinship. I found to be the one place in the world as place of great beauty, family life, edification and faith. A place that I feel is home and I became part of a community. That is no small community and it is like having hundreds of kin's people (from here and in the world now) who simply love and serve each other to the best of their ability. People really care about other people and looking down on someone is a rare event. I cannot remember seeing it happen out on the street. I am only honoured with their company.

Practically I can say peace is a mastered art here and in that I have come to learn the fullness of my passion which is the rights of others and the right of expression for others.

Peace, a theme covered quite extensively herein is a matter which I have always been passionate about. Freedom of the people, embraced with encouragement to succeed is always the possibility in this place we call home, as an immigrant English born person' Raised Up' as Dubliner (North Side) in Ireland.

Of all the things I bear with regard is being welcomed by a nation that has seen so much suffering, of which I have seen a fraction of the effects, and coming from a place where most would have every reason to reject me for my heritage; my heart will never stop aching from the humility of being served to salvation by the same. I have never and will never forget the intimate insights I have gleaned into what it means to be part of that same suffering, welcomed and forgiven all at the same time. I am ever overwhelmed on reflection and to that I was born in to; the way of the Celts, the Irish of love. That way is to love and to serve, in truth of mercy and forgiveness.

I have learned that the Irish are a nation of people that love greatly in peace, free to experience their way of life as they were raised to it – chivalrously. It is a place where everyone is a priest, a prophet and king. To experience this visit any church during any celebrations, weddings, baptisms, funerals or stop by for a chat with any religious of any denomination.

In this place, the Irish have inspired me in everything I have ever done herein and will do, for when there was a lack of understanding as what love is and should be, I have experienced the pinnacle of excellence of how it's done, from the board room to the street. They are the intrinsically gentle spiritual warriors with a clear sense of cultural identity. That I am in love with for it is these wholesome men and women who understand the ways of humanity.

I openly admit to all and one that meanwhile I loved others before I got to Ireland, I had no idea what it was to be loved and that is all another story. Little did I know of ancestral ties which only as I write this have come to light. It explains the sense of familiarity with the nation and with the land that I feel indebted to, attuned to the ages of suffering afflicting the people.

It was Ireland who gave me that impressive insight into all those difficult questions on love, life and faith itself which regardless of one's spiritual place; it determines how we experience this life.

This text is really for everyone who would enjoy a rather untraditional structure of a book as it takes you from place to place in various journeys of understanding in various encounters and reflections which came to pass, that all occurred here in Ireland. They represent both the spiritual and the creative elements of this islands inspiration by being wholly present to the situation. I express views which are for the foundry of literature and poetry for the soul. These are private insights of compassion with the petitions offered at times to furnish deeply forgiving perspectives. I pray it inspires others to visit a new understanding even though it may evoke different from where considerations a comfortable mind may be reluctant to consider.

The interpretation of the text may be unfathomable for it is within we find, actually, we are without. That is what I have discovered when searching my soul. I hope it stirs you interiorly and causes a quest for your soul and reveals the beauty in others souls too. It talks from a range of experiences and all contexts in overcoming the troubled waters of our lives.

Within the flow, I simply hope you find two things if at all from my meagre weak words. Those two things are strength in courage, to be all you are gifted to be. I am reaching out to you. I am telling you these places, there are communities who exist. If you are in a barren world which is doing no more than sucking the life out of you then you have the intuitive power to take action. I am offering you hope in the intuition that you know better really exists...

These are writings produced from various different points of view, addressed to different people at different times (now and in the future) and so meanwhile there is biased and customary addresses to some, I only hope you go into the spirit of the meanings and the depth of the character of some very different prose which carries not necessarily on theme but reflecting on a spectrum of diversity which is in this world.

*The greatest adventure is not that which is outside of us, but all that is **within us**. The villain, that which has held* each and every one of us in bondage, silently using the hands of others who would have alternative plans for us; is not liberation to take on more responsibility, of more this or that. It is when you are freed in conscience to reach the potential of all that you are, so that anything around you are the gifts graced to you and given to you for your life's work. A free conscience is a conscience which can move towards the purpose of your life. Anything else is useless less helpful to anyone around you. Guilt, the aged trap of sin, the tarnish of your soul can be easily polished with your own elbow grease...

Break into your soul and there find the power of love and the presence of peace itself. From there, travel purposefully with all the gifts you have. I say to you, whoever you are; God Bless and ever keep you in his sight, under his wing. I pray always you are at peace with He who loves you more than these meagre words can say.

Come home...

God is full of surprises as well as love and mercy.

I have come to know a few people in Ireland in business, in private lives, education, charity and all faiths. This is dedicated to you bearing up deep respect and deep humility of all the passing conversations and long term relationships which I have made. It is to you I dedicate these reflections, so the world might learn from some of the greatest teachers, by the results of these precious interactions; and recognising those who in the silence of a passing day are simply 'their own family'.

I dedicate my poor effort which is always outshone, to my all those impartial and enduring associates who ensure that human rights are upheld. Human rights are always bound with tension as people come to share the journey of being different humans; we are all human. Their encouragement at times to speak out the truth for the sake of truth has had me do so and for years yet, I pray, those who found my zeal and commitment helpful, that I hold to that same truth.

In total love and joy I dedicate the goodwill of this to the great Irish Saints St Laurence O'Toole and Saint Patrick. Slightly further off, Saint Catherine of Sienna, Saint Anne, Saint Elizabeth, and Saint Padre Pio, Saint Dominic, Saint Francis of Assisi and as I know her 'Our Lady of Mercy' who we are all loved by. In warm affection I offer an assurance that She is Our Mother and to all of us.

To all those who have sincerely loved me, both here and from my distant days this is for you too as I promised I would return with news. This is that delivered and 'highlights' some of the way to go forwards freeing you, dear friends, of what has been those bonds I promised I would find a way of 'cutting' through.

Above all and whom I thank God for the eight who have inspired me and who, without words, I give my endearing affection in prayer, life and after, in service to the accomplishment of World Peace.

Peace be with you all and I ever look forward to happy times spent together again. You are always in my prayers and I am always at your service.

Keep the faith!

Stay in the light!

'kind regards!'

Cēad a milē!

Mille grazie!

Gratias tibi!

Shalom...

Talk Straight, Walk Upright

Peace comes from the wonder of the other. God in the other, that soul, unique and powerful, grace defined in a meeting of moments, the shake of a hand, the first contact of great friendship anticipated.

Love simply interested in mutual understanding, the good of the other. Peace from a place of self security. Abandoning the human response of defence; just holding the will to serve simply making his life easier by 'that one bit'.

Welcoming difference out of interest to grow up and out of love for the sake of others. Only in peace walk faithfully towards a sense of real human experience or enlightenment of the soul.

Ignoring any offence, allowing self to heal – realising the true sacrifice we all face is all our same destiny – that we are actually loved and it is only the disbelief that we are not loved, which in all our encounters of life, in life is the great deception itself.

Freedom of the Heart

All in your heart is the suppression of pain you did not wish to unleash on the world. Oh, noble spirit of man, what glory you offer in imitation of your master, who for sure is in himself pure love. Love which radiates every aspect of your day now and forevermore.

Speak, silent heart of your pain and still calm to suffer gladly the humility of another. Who knows what is asked of your sacrifice of time, of moment of dear affection of your beloved neighbour?

Free your heart to love the lost, the stranger, 'the something' you have come to suspect or judge as an affront to all you have came to stand for?

With reckless abandon offer service to all in your path and rediscover there mystical experience in this existence we call life.

The Affection of a Friend

Friends, known and unknown, seen or unseen are the gifts we can overlook in sense of our day to day experience. We do not necessarily see or value them for what they are until we take the time to share understanding and mutual ground. That is the time taken to love one another for *our differences*.

Here lay the struggle and yet do we not know go on a holiday to submerge ourselves into the culture itself? To experience the sun on a beach not on our street? And as such enjoy the same thing but differently as we do and are? Do we not enjoy watching birds fly because we cannot? Swim because we can? Love because we find beauty in love? Love because that it is divine to love? To care and love as it raises life to everything we are and can be? So then, we ought love all that we *could* love. Always, never missing a chance to be penetrated by such in our selves, nor retain such love we can give to another.

Its' so simple, it's not hard, it is divine...

A
Procession
of Peace

1) Forgive first and let's face this together it's
   going to hurt someone, somehow and
   probably you and your pride. Space made to
   be filled instead with grace... All
   communications are flawed with prejudice,
   normally our own.

2) Welcome the person, whole heartedly. Be
   honest in your expressions. No hiding how
   one may feel. Take permission now to say

aloud to anyone 'I don't understand', 'that hurt' and 'I will pray about that...' Praying and thinking are one and the same discourse to recourse to the greater good of any person, including yourself. Time well spent praying has prevented the need for more cures...

3) Find your pleasantries. All relations have different rhythms. Never mind the law or worrying about the accusation of friend turned foe. These things are boundaries often which if one makes no complaint against hold no weight! Here is where friendship and trust marry the souls of nations in the art of forgiveness itself. Instead of focussing on what you cannot, seek what you can. Stack the odds so that in all times every relationship flourishes within its own cultural rules and boundaries. This can only happen when one understands the need soften other and attempts (you only have to attempt) to assist them in some meaningful way. It does not

have to be your work, you can simply refer or promote a cause, with reasonable consent.

4) Relax and trust in negotiating the common ground. Two people speaking different languages can still smile at each other and still feel that bond of commonality – they are human with needs. Both still eat and drink.

5) Honesty in exchange. Be fair, be honest and hold onto your integrity. That will be different to your actual and spiritual age. Thus, know you can encounter fifteen year olds with far greater integrity than you and you will bend to bless them with your humility. That humility they may lack and in such encounters there are divine negotiations, divine love and divine intervention. Allow God to move you together in his power and He really will!

Self-Esteem

Self-esteem and self-confidence are modern expressions of life today. Some of us may say you are to simply be and why not be, who you are completely with acceptance of humility and abandonment to selflessness. Not being hard, be soft in heart and mind, in will and community.

'Love saves lives...'

St John Damascene

It's Not Hard

Create a real community or your things to do *and* allow them to. Reduce interference by not allowing anything other than organic growth in all that is legal, moral and ethical. That is all that ever needs doing.

Gentle Humility

A means to flow within the course of life,

without disrupting your good friend.

Why is peace so difficult
to accomplish?

Because most people
suspect it is not possible.

Faith is the solution to this,
that *'it is'* possible.

Play with Peace

Players, play on peacefully,

every soul!

But play like children, for innocence
only brings joy to the mother when
she reads a poem or ponders the
divine scribbling of her child.

Scribble

Practise Everything Safely

If I could offer one piece of advice it would be this.

Practise everything safely.

In good humour make it your only ambition to receive the best and most beneficial for your time and experience, in accordance to your life purpose and the delivery of your life gifts.

This way you will have life to the full and be filled with the Holy Spirit who wants to move you.

The Mystery of Evil

The mystery called 'evil' is a verb describing something that opposes our beliefs, morally, ethically and any other 'ology's' or 'ism's' or 'ist's'. What is good to one is not to another and on encounter the resistance may be presented as 'evil' to one or the other. There is no mystery we simply have a choice in our behaviours. We act out of stupidity or ignorance if we participate with the knowledge that we are going against our conscious.

It is a mystery not that evil can and does exist on a theological level in any circumstance to do with a human. We are indeed afflicted with that called original sin. The mystery is when we are not ignorant that we stupidly participate in the self harm of doing it.

Is It Okay To Read The Notes in this Book

or Will You Eat Me?

Zen masters are notoriously disciplined often using methods revealed by their 'Lady' for centuries.

Therefore, Zen students wash out your bowl after breakfast or you may have to learn what is meant by:

'the unlifted book cannot be taken by the thief in the night'

This is Zen speak for loving the students current level not their underestimation of themselves that these pitiful words are all they can learn from.

Ways to Nurture Peace in Your Community

1) What you don't have is ideas...right? Here's how it has been proven for centuries to work without using technology. The essential component of tech free experiences is a prime opportunity being missed by most organisations.

2) Create community projects with end dates. Rapid response and fast initiatives which are given with one or two objectives in mind to answer an immediate need. These initiative must come from within the community and not be imposed on a community.

3) Congratulate your community leaders and show them some accolade with pleasant emails from time to time. Inspire them and let them know what you need. This will bring you things you need and not be told what you can have.

4) Outreach to the sick, ill, abandoned and isolated. Take them things they might appreciate and talk about old memories. Show them that they are loved and valued. These are the most important people in our society.

5) Stop demanding from public sources everything you need. There is a reality and a strain that only everyone can take. Therefore, act in your community, be raised up by them. Lean on their support and solve the problems so that it is the people that power the places. If you need a good example, get on a plane, and visit the Citizens Information Centres in Dublin or ask any local on the streets of Dublin (really, they'll nearly take you there!).

6) If you are in a position to charge rent, fund mortgages and so on. Be fair, take less and design products which will give the best value for everyone. Add in month off breaks and increase the well being of people. Become popular and increase by many margins. Create a statement if you are a mass stakeholder and a Mexican wave by instead of increasing, set a new trend by decreasing the rate one month and increase in your own business. Be loved by your guests and you will always be well regarded.

7) Develop initiatives which allow parents to control curriculums. Give power to people and let them inform you how they want THEIR child rearing. We are all born free and not anyone's property or responsibility. They have Human Right to live free form interference. Realise that that the pressure on schools affects parents and children are being denied their right not only of childhood but to their parents themselves. Do everything by conference at a local level encouraging generous verbal involvement so that economy and politics regains its own respect.

8) Bring back the community activity. Mobile libraries, the pop van, the milk deliveries and post people. There was once even a chip van. Come away from the national brands and start to focus on local people, local skills, local incomes. Enhance the value of the community.

9) Outreach central directory service by phone. Create a service where anyone can call and explain their problem and immediately they can get local support booked, networked and so on. This is an idea longing to come to life. A great help to all businesses big and small.

10) Befriending services to the elderly and the isolated. Ensuring that they feel part of a network *should they wish.*

11) Free Tea – really. Free tea/coffee stops signposted for all civil service personal no matter the role or rank. Given by businesses with limitations on how many per week per place. Give back to these people who are often underpaid and heavily criticised for not meeting actually impossible targets. Boost their morale and boost your respect as business. Win their interest and invite them in, they might appreciate that and you will benefit.

12) Hire people or involve people with a 'record'. Penance served it's no longer anyone's business to carry on the judgement. A community holding someone to passed deeds only inspires passed deeds. Immerse them in mercy and they will become mercy. People, who are loved, do not offend. Think about it.

13) Start and run small and large competitions for art, drama, best pet and so on. Recognise the upcoming and small people who really are doing great things –

that is they are making an effort to become what they were designed to be.

14) For civil service staff, volunteers and charity workers. Start bi-annual awards with cash prizes. If you are a major employer – give official recognition to your people. Give them meaningful prizes such as cash.

15) Businesses – share your profits. If you want success in this life what you will do is increase your staff retention and achievement by actually recognising them ALL. Splitting end of year profits is one way this can happen. Leadership and the recovery of wealth will no longer come by constantly fleecing your people in the knowledge of fleshy profits. What it will come by is the respect and stabilisation of your people who will do such a great job you cannot be short of profit.

16) Local funders. These are local funds held by committees or organisations which can simple provide funds for services to do with private health or animal health matters. No lengthy process and maybe only one time help points this alone will help ease pressure all over the place.

17) Community Awards – community people electing community people in relation to special efforts made, often unnoticed, unrecognised things like delivering someone's baby or helping them through a difficult time.

18) Amnesty's. People don't want to continue their old ways sometimes. They have no way out. Amnesty's where they can be rid of anything safely is a great way of starting anew and fairly with people in this world. We recycle batteries so why not anything else?

19) Free holistic healthcare and well being days. Simply set up and serve everyone. Not pointing out it's for the labelled homeless, the labelled business person or civil worker. The world has had enough of categories and labels. It is what is causing the problems in the main because it type casts and stereo types. Fact, we are all human and being that we can all fall badly on hard and terrible times, never knowing when or where out next meal might come from; get passed labels to not caring. See the soul and serve the person. Indifference is dangerous as what it will do is not help you when you need it most. Even if right now

you believe you are blessed with every person and thing you need.

20) Remember the Workers. Remember the employed and the self employed, who are perpetually overlooked. Seen as the staple income of countries and actually the ones working the hardest to provide for the country, furnishing money to contribute to a society, which may seem to them give them very little in return. Find ways of showing that even if it is only a mean for two at the end of the year. More needs to be done to show actually, you do care.

21) Remember, we all matter and we all can have effect as a community, a nation, a country, a union, as an organisation and all else. These voices matter and they deserve to be heard in full, not part and all communities valued as the culture they are. Respect customs honourably with an open heart and a willingness to listen and the desire to understand. To help when it's asked for so that all suffering is minimised with almost immediate effect.

22) Visit Ireland for a week, schedule appointments ahead to seek 'go see' advice from any expert available. It will be some of the best insight you ever receive in business, politics, education and family life.

Cease Hurt, See Beauty

We humans are evermore living longer and longer.
Now is the time in everything we do, everything...to
cease hurt and see beauty. Every moment of our lives
should be scattered with beauty and if not we ought
be beautifying it with great acts of charity, love and
mercy. The world and all its people has see enough
pain. It ends when we cease hurt and see beauty. It
starts with us and eventually there can be no reason to
have any one anywhere justify action where others
face the horror of actions someone else made. This is
the way to peace.

(Written from St Saviours Church, Dominic Street, Dublin, Ireland,
Inspired by Saint Dominic)

'Beloved Priest'

Dear priest, please know in union with His Mother, Jesus performed His first miracle at Cana. Until then He Himself, may not have known who He was born to be, neither may you, beloved Son.

Therefore as asked, do and see how you turn water into wine, and how no priest has ever done a single thing without his mother who says:

"Do as He tells you to do..."

Gossip *and* Grass

Gossip nor grass neither be, nor persuader of others, nor informant, nor betrayer become. Be as the grass bending in the wind, in the light find glorious and true all that is you.

If in doubt, leave it out!

Love the Lead

Love the lead of your life, the Holy Spirit found for some in the sacred church flowing effortlessly from the Holy Sacrament we call the Mass and in receiving the Eucharist.

 Should you not know what here we speak, it is opportune that you follow those feet.

Ask...

Just Stop

Quit, acquit, and forgive all that may ever stand in the way of all that in the glory of your hours. These days passing, rejoice and love all that you might never remember, for we will and do forget all that has passed. Our ungrateful memory which fails us in times of need, ever our conscience which demands us the fulfilment of all we could receive in the faith of all that is, unseen, unmoved.

(Written at the National Gallery of Ireland)

Err to Learn

In all we do, err to learn and swift to learn thoust will be. In the days that pass by reflect upon your mistakes and either teach or learn them. An example is not always so obvious in all they do and when and how. It is so they, like Christ, do what they have to do in order to get done what must be done, in that there is the wind of change.

(written at the Garden of Remembrance, Dublin)

The only truth is the gospel truth which beyond words is between the lines reaching into imagination and history.

Deep into our flesh and living within us, the means to relate to a wealth of knowledge which should we walk in the truth, we might come to know it.

If we look to the Great Orator and Life's Author, can it then only be true we become it?

The Mysterious Power of the

Rosary Versus the 'Other Side'

If 'this' represented the 'other thing' then this is what the Rosary does. Thus we do not need to raise our eyes or vocalise our prayers at times. We need to focus of the mystery of God's works.

47

On Talents

What a man lacketh in talent,

he can make up in generosity.

(Written at St Stephens Green, on the grass at the right of
the main gate by the Luas stop)

Art appreciation Course. I wonder if people know how to 'appreciate' art at all?

(Pause)

And still a child teaches us by reaching...

(Think)

Standing in the presence of master, silence teaches us interiorly to hear their thoughts left interiorly in the space which can only be felt by those who have the reverence to know. There only the Mass; there is only the master. 'There' is love.

(Also written at the National Gallery, Dublin, Ireland)

Spiritual Defence Manifest Material Protection

The Rosary is the most powerful defence against the 'Other Thing' for he flees...

All that we do in the physical is a reflection of that we do in the spiritual (unless of course one knows the sacred footprints).

So, out pray it and cease any physical intervention. We are of peaceful warriorship of the spiritual.

Leave in the hands of God and our Lady of Mercy, all things.

Anything we can accomplish with our hands should be done by praying the Rosary binding our hands together in those most moving beads of promised hope.

We can do with the Rosary all that needs to be done, if we honestly *only* offer it to Our Lady.

Do not be pleased at the losses of any other when He casts them from their throne to raise you the lowly, but remain lowly. Even when they do evil things and we have witnessed the response of God and we know it is He Himself who acts in the Holy Spirit. Do not rejoice for it is not Holy to turn ones back from thine enemy and not pray. It is not wise to gloat or be proud, for who performed the wonder. You think you? Then if so get behind yourself dear self sabotaging foe of your own soul.

Yes, make them lifetime strong, your Rosary. Yes, hold them during communion or have them about you in all circumstances. Lest do you know what gift you hold, that which serves you without your request to even ask. You chain of office recognised by Angels of God and feared by the fallen angels. With your Rosary you need nothing more than to know they are there, they are with you.

Do not use them as a weak expression of faith. A trinket? Let me stand you corrected. Pray on them I urge you for the loss of faith is as recoverable as loss of youth. In the time of your life, enhance the depth of the mystery in such gift of life and become that which was you baptised as Priest, Profit, King.

The art is this! Should you ask a worthless opinion of such a magnificent affair in the sight of God. *All we ever do is in the act of faith or act in the faith of prayer, which all happens in the spiritual.* There is the way to happiness for if prayed contritely, never will you face the sacrifice that He had to make, for unto children are revealed 'the secrets' of the Rosary and the secrets revealed keep you safe. Listen, follow and respond to that whispers of God who called your soul to rest in Him. The Father defends the child and the one who does not *is not.*

The Quest

'The quest to find the answer is as fruitless as the barren ocean of doubt.

Treasure is always found in the unseen depths of the world... '

Oh Divine Master

The Sleeping man at the Blessed Sacrament is a living testimony to the trust we should reflect in Christ Jesus. An unappreciated grace of simple trust in 'He' 'His Lord' is watching over him in the depth of his contemplative prayers.

Lost in the interior of his soul with the angels and saints at that most glorious throne, we do not come to contemplate...behold we are taught again the fine lesson of what Christ revealed about children. And so, we should not prevent them from ever coming to him but rather, fling open the doors in our hearts, so that we might have the eyes to see, all that the sleeping man obtains in his most humble of prayers.

(Written at the Blessed Sacrament Chapel, Bachelors Quays
Dublin, Ireland)

Ideals and Idols

What has this world come to that I see the realisation of worshipping false idols. I hear their cries and complaints, their deep interior despairs. Yet, drawn away these are to life destroying ideals. Ideals, such last as chaff on a winter night. Maybe of use in brief, a flicker of light which for a moment gives it's heat and then is gone. It leaves them abandoned, cold, without warmth. They suffer somehow and how we hurt too.

God the Father is not such a source of goodness He forgets to stoke up the Flame Eternal; not the flame dissipated. He will forevermore, with those creatures who know him, come ever more generous for imitating His son, and as such, redeem His Son.

The false idols will rot in time among the countless effigies of guise which have already become dust. You, Child of God, Child of Mine, you are here in my heart and will be remembered in Heaven and on Earth.

(Written at the Blessed Sacrament Chapel, Bachelors Quays
Dublin, Ireland)

The Sorrowful Heart

What I meditate on most, as human alone, is
what and how did St Peter care for Our Lady
after the crucifixion of Jesus Christ. Did he
himself hold her, have the words to say? And
then what of St John who was told 'Behold
your Mother?' Did he too take some service in
her pangs, never fading pain? Did she ever
come to love and embrace them as her sons?
At all?

These things I wonder for how overcoming the
grief of loss and from where does one take
strength when the father, husband are gone
and into the fate of widowhood she stepped?

They Are yet To Believe...

If it is hard to believe He is there, why is it so hard to believe He is there? I do not know how to unbelieve all that is revealed. Maybe it is doubt of consecration.

I pray that all who gaze upon the Blessed Sacrament come, even if only just once, to see with their own hearts the living truth of Who is really there, in front of them.

I pray too that they move their hearts, bodies and souls so that they may for all their natural lives know the way home and stay true to the path that He calls them down.

Zen and Religion

Does it Suit Catholicism?

In my humble opinion; one in unity with the Holy Spirit, quietly understands without resisting interior or exterior resistance to:

'Be still and know I am God'

(Psalm 46)

Then yes, it is suited if One in unity with the Holy Spirit understands Zen. Zen, however, may never understand Catholicism.

What Is It To Understand?

It is to;

a) Be able to uphold and explain your subject matter at the level of intellect to whom you are speaking;

b) To look up at such in the graciousness given to you so that you glorify God's work and not your own.

Sovereign Divine

Not one of us, Christian, can argue the divine sovereignty of Christ. That is the answer to becoming peace keepers with each other. To hold in admiration all wisdom, beauty and knowledge being assured that He who shepherds us is authentic, reliable and walked this earth in truth; causing still the living history of His work on Earth.

What more then is He in Heaven if this is His accomplishment on Earth?

In Christ all Christians are bound to the loving, most merciful Word.

Are We Alone?

No. I do wonder at times the world (the West) sometimes. It has been over analysed and over explained so much no one can come to anything agreeable (variable terms in different languages, for example).

In short, all faiths, all religions have 'identified' communications with superior intelligences over all history consistently.

I stand by the angels and saints as I have no other explanation for what we call 'supernatural' grace other than, whoever made that possible, without technology, clearly is super intelligent. I call Him God.

In this case, I can only suggest that one 'encounters' all this themselves, as that is the only way one can and will believe. Existentially, one may learn; by watching.

Holy Spirit and the Writers Pen

Dear Beloved Holy Spirit,

Your love of me has me write to you for them.

Show them your way, secret and divine, before Our Lord Jesus Christ in the most Holy Sacrament on the Altar.

Let them brave step with you behind them. Show them to take in the mass or greeting cards to start, and there write out their message; blessed in the sight of Our Lord Glorified so that your invisible trail might lead others home.

It's a small dream of mine I wish to share, so that they might know it was you, who made me care.

I entrust them to you, guide.

Amen

Brief Advice for Mystics

If you want to be a mystic, I can tell you now, you are probably not. You are instead dazzled by an attraction which is drawing you away from God and not to Him. Meditate on this.

Those who **want** to be counsellors, may need counselling. Those who **want** to be officers, of one kind or another, may want authority (typically). Those who **want** to be mystics may need the assurance of God's wonders made clear.

Asking a child what they **want** to be when they grow up is a question flawed in an unstable frame. Ask instead *"what will you do with your gifts when you are older?"* and suddenly there is a vista epic. A life worth living...

Real counsellors, mystics or officers are given the grace into their hearts so that it might serve others. One cannot 'want' for it will not be given. One cannot be filled if one is filled with want. One gets what one is given by God as talent and is expected to, multiply it. Grace dispensed in the emptiness as our supplicated will to Him.

Mystics, have guts not unlike the doctors and surgeons of this world mortal. They face Holy Fear in piety knowing exactly what it costs them and others in life *and* in death. Meditate on this carefully and do not stray into ungoverned or unapproved ways not of your culture or your heritage. You have no right to appropriate it, nor sacramental rite to act on it. It therefore is not safe and thus you will suffer all that you draw and delay in all that you were sent for. Mediate on this too – very carefully.

Know thyself as thy enemy and you will come close to knowing what really is stealing your attention so that you become deprived of your given and hidden gifts.

Serve God and all wonders happen. It's that simple – let it be, 'fiat!'

Unspoken Gratitude

Dear Holy Spirit,

Through you I have seen the beginning of humankind's salvation. Trodden down until now, hand up in every nation, at near, in all places I have seen your works.

This short note is to thank you, for always proceeding from the Father to the Son and from the Son, to us; the undeserving.

We have not struggled as our ancestors did, for we see and have you here. Enlighten us.

Our poor affection returned ungratefully in your sight in meagre gratitude.

Thank you,

All Humanity

Honesty

Why people do not ask you for your honesty is because they can always be challenged on the same. This is a test of society and one that practises forgiving and forgetting will love and ignore all that is forgiven. However, we are now so overwhelmed by open communications (in the West and some of the East of the year 2019), we are set to fail.

A wise soul knows this and takes on the truth of Calvary and forgiveness, repentance. To be sorry and seek forgiveness for all that you have most definitely done. This is not as hard as it seems, truly.

I pray that you are cared for by the Seat of Wisdom and in that providence prove we all have a lot more to live for than the falling for the deceit that is made for our demise.

May you assist and protect us, Our Lady of Mercy in this life and stand upon the throat of that serpent.

On Enemies

Enemies and I will refer only to my own, I pray for them; privately as a rule. It is what I am taught and hold firm to. I can say I have had some worthy adversaries. I still pray for those who acted alone or as Jesus Christ taught, for those who acted as a group too. I pray for their salvation, petition for their souls and if I know them, those who have offended me – I am only grateful they revealed themselves so I could act in accordance to that fine and noble teaching, to forgive ones enemies.

My advice, based on a lifetime's privileged experience of eating with those most people would sooner bring before judgement – forgive and forget, that is the greatest gift given to you and therein the substantial advice of the great Saint Sister Faustina too.

I am not searching for God.

I am showing you how to find Him

(Go through Our Lady and Angel Gabriel)

On Possibility

What can I tell you without coming from promises of discretion, or privacy, or confidentiality? Nothing. I can only assure you that in all I do and all I have witnessed, is and has come from God as miracles and wonders that even the experts are left aghast at. That is because God has a plan, He sends the right people at exactly the right time and those who are in the right places listen and respond to use their given station all the glory of God's hand. You can be an instrument of God if you will only sing His Song...You have within you all that you need to be able to do and witness the same.

I am a poor witness to you who can say only the truth and that is God made it possible with me. There is hope for everyone if he chose not only a tainted, beaten and rejected instrument but one who had no reason aside years of silent instruction, to trust in all that I could not see. Do!

Peace is the most powerful means and in the silence *everything* can be heard.

The Most Zenish Thing

You Ever Said?

St Saviours Servers Prayer

✝ (V) Lord, we are not worthy, not fit to serve you;

(R) Who art goodness alone.

(V) Lord, we are nought without your abounding love;

(R) Which animates all life.

(V) Lord, bless us with your Mercy, inspired for Your flock;

(R) You call as we pray.

(Examination of conscience 3 minutes – 1 minute meditating each of the above)

✝ (V) Lord, we beg your forgiveness to wash clean our hearts;

(R) Free our minds to yours inclined, alone.

(V) Fill us to spill with *St Dominic's humility* that we may assist in these living works;

(R) This font of life.

(V) Lord, watch far from the boundaries of these walls; let your dewfall, cascade afar.

(R) Put man and beast to bed, fortify your faithful and inspire your living souls.

(V) Bring us home, Lord, our simple petition;

(R) Bring us home Lord - in life, in death.

(V) Keep safe this ancient city;

(R) Our ancient love of you.

(V) Protect your priests, inflame their hearts;

(R) *to praise, to preach, to bless.*

(V) All this do under your Mothers Mantel, from within the folds of Her Holy Veil;

(R) Make them docile and wise; in love.

Concluding Petition (Said together)

† We ask all this, knowing our worthlessness for our sins, placing all our trust in the arms of Our Lady of Mercy; that She may dry the tears of others, in the neglect of our presence to them.

O Lord, guide us in this Holy Prayer of the Mass. Permit us to Love as you will us to Love; Completely, Selflessly, Absolute.

Amen

†

A Prayer Before Despair

†

Lord, my hands are tied so free my soul
to bless,

Within my breast, let me lay with you at
rest.

†

Amen

The Lost Priests Prayer

†

You called me by name Lord. You have brought me here before you, Gentle Judge.

For you sanctified my hands. No human touch in consecration. As you promised, like Your Father, You left me with freewill.

Remember your Mercy O God, O Christ Jesus, O Redeemer.

I have offended You Beloved Redeemer, I condemn myself in your presence. I have adorned myself in sins which drove off all that you drew close.

I have scattered your flock, taken innocence and used illusionary power for influence. It was not given to me. I stole it in exchange for tattered apparel.

I wanted them to love me, desire me; and this is my sin. This is my fault, my thrice fold evil the desecration of consecration.

I took back my freewill as prize. That which I offered up in imitation of you; instead to only imitate the faithless master, who is not worthy of name.

Hell would not have me for this betrayal. Purgatory an existence I relate now, a glimpse of hope in sight of salvation in your plan for Man.

Humiliate me Lord Jesus, show me all that I am. You all your given life made it clear; to walk on. I meandered, Lord. I meandered.

In my way laying I was caught by distraction. In thought, then word, then deed. I sought from the world the ecstasy of you; for my flesh would not wait in diligent suffering to bear the fruit of patience.

I revolted in being tamed, co-heir to the scars of human servitude. Forgive them and accept my repentance for them; should they not speak of your Great Mercy in their grave states.

No man can comfort me. No food relinquishes its taste. No thirst quenched or peace within; without. Your Grace I deny at Your Banquet. My conscious accuses me before you. I fail to trust in Your Mercy.

I hide in my disgrace. In its bidding doubt says "He does not love you". I remain chained and out stretched – torn asunder in this rampage of the soul. This silent suffering alone cries out to you, dwelling in this spiralling chaos of a haunted existence.

In strutting amongst the flocks I have seen that thing between me and you. I am afraid, Lord Jesus. That thing is me. I am a man and I have been weak, arrogant, fooled and foolish. I am afraid of my kin, my neighbour and my superior.

I fear temptation and your Holy Spirit. This Holy Fear the revealed gift of my offences. You, true to Word offer that living proof of goodness still. Oh, how You strike true with the same light Saint Paul came to fall for.

Take these obstructions from our union. These fears I have manifested without your name. Blaze it in your Divine Fires and set me alight in faith. Take from my view that which praises you not, so that I may recourse as witness of your Unfathomable Mercy.

Possess me *only* to think of You.

Make my superiors merciful in their wisdom to knowing only you have the right and the power to take me broken upon your shoulders; do not let them stumble at the same temptation that leads to all human cruelty. No one can imitate Your Justice without Your Mercy; this lesson learned from this sin.

Lord, You let Judas go, You did not stop him. His guilt had him leave. I have no right to ask, nor to receive. No right to stay and nor to leave.

I ask you this from Your Most Merciful Heart and with the Saints and Angels, seek their intercession, as per your will for me.

I beg you, do not let me go; without You.

Remember your Mercy O God, O Christ Jesus, O Redeemer *in all I ever have, is You.*

†

Amen

The Meadow

Understand the teacher,
understand the man.

The meadow asks not what the
butterfly does.

Read Between the Lines

("There is always something going on" - Hot Fuzz)

_____

_____

_____

_____

_____

Gentlemen!

And, this sirs! Is the miracle. That we do not machine to do it! Nor training, nor education. For what we accomplish by faith is of God.

The use of imagination is not of use to education where it dissolves the gaze... That *is* straight at the cross, to the Risen Christ, whom should he wish reveal the way, you see Him.

Maturity

Maturity is not a process
we can interfere with.
God alone decrees this.

Hence, He taught them in
the temple by question
and listening before His
days would start...

Negotiators Mastery

For Experts and the Experienced

Whoever you are and whatever you do. YOU contribute to peace in the world and peace in other people's hearts. It you get in a rut and find yourself an advocate or a mediator, here is the best of what I have learnt.

Step 1: Call an immediate pause – commit to inaction.

Step 2: Appoint a nice location and arrange tea, coffee, water, and fresh pressed juices.

Step 3: Forgive any childish antics and offer mutual apologies.

Step 4: Agree to help solve each other's problem. No questions asked, cost free to aid the others solutions.

Step 5: Refuse to undertake any action which causes harm, in any way to human life, ecology or the country's economy. Even if you are working at a local level consider this carefully.

Step 6: Create a shared plan of mutual effort and end courage the fostering of fraternity.

Step 7: Set a date to celebrate successful points of the journey.

Step 8: Use experienced counsel and advise others in the same – creating historic noble leaders, who save the world. This has never been achieved before; is a worthy adventure.

"We are as in death as we are in life..."

(Inspired by a dream with Saint Thomas Aquinas)

Alms Giving

Giving financial gifts may not be the most charitable or profitable thing you can do with the same amount of time.

Smiling at a child might be.

They suffer in silence.

Advice That I would Offer anyone?

Do it Like

A Pro! ©

(Really... no matter what you are doing.)

At the Table

Tip: Three things never to discuss at a dinner table.

1. Matters pertaining to any sexual relations.
2. Politics – yours or anyone's.
3. Religion – yours or anyone's.

When one is in excellent company, the way to keep it is by showing your personality. Your personality has nothing to do with those three things above if you ever want to finish a meal in peace and end the day with an easy conscience.

The Paramount Vocations

Peace Keeper, Peace Maker. These are the two paramount vocations of which we can all take our part, in pairs or switch about in situ. Never the two should face other in adversary stances. Both would surely perish. Shoulder to shoulder they become the passage of peace, rod and staff; guide and light to those in distress and harm's way. Whichever you are, become that you are called to in your humanity. You are called.

Simple understanding when with a friend in any situation, start to see how much together with such a simple understanding how such a troubled world starts to become fairer, just, less strained. This is because the good in whatever you do excels 'beyond the action of your time', in time.

Peace keepers a silent unspoken strength rooted firmly in their experience of surviving various conflicts and disappointments in life. They bear the secret knowledge of suffering and as a rock in the road of perdition stand firm to offer some resistance so that a soul can pause and discern. Without words they speak volumes, sheltering their found soul briefly, giving enough time for them to think.

Interiorly they pursue their selves and accost them by the throat demanding that part of them is transformed to love through the wisdom of introspection and with their Lord, bring that part to judgement. Resolved, absolved they are apparently fearless and interiorly terrific. They are of solid faith.

Peace Makers. These are as the gentle whispers of a warm night with fragranced air. Uttered prayers, gentle considerations flow from them of hope and sound direction with no motive aside the love, they know is given to them, in trust of sharing to the needy.

The manifest wonder workers of life, they stitch together the scraps of the soul with the softest of silk and white raiment they make, fit for the glorious high tables.

The resources, are what they find about them, what they are given to share with. Their cause and delight is to be in awe at the wonder of His works. Their plan, the salvation of what soul lay before them. Their strength is charity which is self giving in style and nature. Their generosity and faithful devotion to assist in multiplying abundance their sign of grace, distinguished.

These are the *paramount vocations* of which any of us can participate in at any time. We are simply that as our highest expression of humanity and it is often there amongst that work we find we experience the ecstasy of joy, happiness, harmony for the longest brief moments of our lives.

One needs not apply for a vocation that they already hold. One may indeed have to apply themselves to the vocation that they have been fully dressed to act in.

Peace Keepers,

Peace Makers.

Thank you.

Stuck in the Rut

A rut occurs when two great stags (male deer) lock horns and apply force in the same direction at each other. It is their way of working out who is the best for breeding. Eventually they have to work together to get out of it, or become prey to the weather or hunters or worse (to them) their herd leads off without them. Then, with no effort some young handsome buck shows up and takes over with not so much as a scratch of effort made in rutting.

This is the same problem when you are engaged in a career or in parenting situation which you know is making you a hypocrite on philosophical or religious grounds. Well, radical pressure calls for radical action. Your family and your career are the two most important responsibilities you have. Any interference in either of them should be taken seriously.

Radical means greatly different to the status quo (or norms) that you have been groomed into thinking is acceptable. This comes from many directions I leave out here, as we are actually very talented in knowledge as to what those may be today. Norms, they take away choice and freedom at such high a level one may yield out of fear alone. Do not fear, seek and find...

Suggestion: Take a piece of paper and note down what you want to happen and then be open to the world showing you new ways. This may mean not relying on the internet but actually going to speak to other people and discover what they do instead. Then, find out what best suits you and work out the advantages to it. Make a *concerted decision* and follow the course you have just set.

Welcome to happiness...

A Secret from Diplomacy

Never have a dog in the fight.

Leave them at the door.

Then drink tea.

(...or coffee when you are with friends)

On Succeeding with the Delusion of Defeat

Understand quickly this. No matter whom you are and what you do, people with different attitudes will support you on the way through...

Look out for them and take the gifts that are helpful for you...

Meditate on that and then do it.

That is how easy it is...

Then, gentle person, you are close to God and God is close to you.

Peace brethren.

Cease pain, see beauty.

Drink Tea

(or Coffee with friends)

How Will I Know?

Dearest Mystical Student,

This is not a question at all. It is rooted in relativism. You look back for material fact. That, dearly beloved student of the mystical walk with God, is not prudent of your energy. It is better not to care than to look back. I reiterate this constantly I know. If you so missed the Easter lectures of 2019, I spoke out. A reminder "No one knows the day or hour..." (Jesus)

Now, if you are trapped or snared by your interest in self validation or validation of God you accomplish quite admirably the errors of violating the commandment 'thoust shalt not test God'. Thus, no slow walk to judgement for your backs to God, your life's last breath faded, taken by surprise. One cannot face God neither repose. Thus so, we always pray for a peaceful and provided death, true? This is one reason why. Therefore, do not ask questions like *how will I know?* God is your judge and grace given to you by the measure you can be readied for. So be willing, open, ready.

Serve and you will be given the grace to serve with. Face the cross and do not rush to fade into those wounds. Be grateful we you can kneel at the foot of the cross and *too* on the other side. You know what you know. It's enough assurance.

Pray or out pray! But pray!

The Concluding Prayer

of Fatima

†

Oh Divine Mother, We thank you for your maternal protection and guidance over these years.

We thank you for all the joys of safety and assurance of well being during the moments we nearly despaired.

With your divine and tender love, ever watch over us and seal into the past all that you told us of, so that we may remain safe within your gaze, under your mantel of protection, of not just us but the entire human family.

†

The People Who You Must Let Pass You By

There are certain unavoidable matters in life that you must come to understand as you progress through your purpose and into your providential destiny. The first thing to remember no matter what you are experiencing the reality is you have some experience of it anyway...

For example, when you walk down the street you walk by people, correct? You don't feel guilty about not greeting every one of them or keeping in contact, remembering birthdays and on. Do you?

Therefore, being destined to be part of a greater plan, this is a reality you will face and the size of the experience becomes ever greater as all the flashes of experience that you have are built upon as the small bricks of the road that silently, the angels lay straight before you...

Define what is

'Culture of Death'?

In my experience of the violation of human rights across many different places. It is, in my humble opinion;

'Any contributory action that leads to any consequence which in <u>some way</u> takes away the dignity of any human's rights or a human's ability of self expression, that diminishes the accomplishment of any potential or actual realisation of what it is to be themselves as fully human in life'

Where anyone coerces, controls, manipulates any other in the accessibility of their rights, in any situation whether considered legal or not does not take away the offence, nor the damage to that person, spiritually, physically, psychologically. In anyway...

There is no equivalent compensation and it is nor is any injury repairable without scar. Few relationships recover the dent of doubt.

Anger, fear, rage, revenge all stem from these degrading 'consequences'. The perpetrator finds themselves at risk of outrage either in spiritual or by material manifest repercussions.

To avoid this, take a stand. Be the person who refuses to participate in the *helplessness* of another and be the person who empowers or protects the other.

Any use of the terms 'it's policy', 'it's the rules', 'it's how we do things' – that is a red flag. They arise from their own depressed position to use you as their footstool. Nay say you to such, you are for the purpose you were sent for not being at the foot of less than your God.

Where there are hard set institutional or systematic procedures or protocols, the best thing one can often do *is not* participate at all. Plan an exit strategy for yourself and leave that place - resign. Make a concerted conscious choice to cause the effect of your presence to be better spent elsewhere.

The Culture of Death *takes* many operatives. You may be one of them. By not participating you actively participate instead in the 'Culture of Life' and there you will find not only peace, but joy and harmony, which is the anticipated bliss you cannot have in the marriage to the Culture of Death. Buy into the Culture of Life and convert in your heart from the Culture of Death which has certainly mistaken you for a fool.

Meditate on

these

things...

On the Definition of Love...

The **greatest gift** of being human is the art made in the recognition of love, not just as other, but in the whole of humanity...

Let Me Pass Friends Internationalē

It is hard being impartial. This is the laser focus of the peacekeeper. That is one who loves everyone for all that they are and is willing to restrain vested interests in themselves, so that another can fully express their identity. It is so that many people have sat with others aware of their so called differences on the matters of the day so peace can remain. This is to love as I was taught to love and hard taught at that.

Peace Keepers keep the peace and make it happen as a Peace Maker, often quietly praying away. I pray things get better for you and whatever you are in, that you find that hand to lead you to safety. You are loved and *you are* worth that effort.

We are Men and Women of great faith even without religion, if we want it that way. That is to say that we are bound in the historic blood of all our predecessors who, for us all gave up life to call us their successors. That life, to us all means something, that we are unified in the effort of our ancestors – whoever they are. Not one of us anywhere who desires prosperity ought be tempted to disbelieve such virtuous camaraderie does not share in its fraternity. It does.

Our spirit, those who were held in suppression, oppression, serfdom, afflicted by some kind, is mutual hurt. It is transformed as a mutual time line of divine passion. Such is a *mighty united understanding* of fellowship; this is our brother and sisterhood, even if sometimes we fail to recognise one another as such kinsfolk.

Freedom of the spirit is the wind that will cut through mountains and bring us to pastures fresh. That is where we meet as friends, together. That's Ireland!

We all want to know peace and to *express ourselves* authentically as ourselves. Our meeting place is the epicentre of understanding that *we are free*, born free and freedom is more than a state of mind, it is *our state of life.*

I praise God for you and never will you walk alone when with a friend of God.

Thank you...

A Petition to the Sisterhood

To My Sisters who are beloved in the ways of the woman, the Divine Female. This is my petition to you. By the Grace of God, may you find truth and strength in these words. I mean only to speak to your gentle feminine prowess.

I hear you say 'it' is for your well being that you consent. I understand the pain, the problem, whatever the circumstances. I feel the affliction myself, for I am a woman and I have had to think the same thoughts because that is what we are **told** to consider. That is the way of the West – the wild west. We are given all these 'considerations' enshrined in law which makes it apparently guilt free. What a lie that **might** be. You are unique and you will experience the effects as you uniquely will. They cannot be predicted nor prescribed. Only you know you and you have the exclusive right to decide of your own volition.

I have no right to ask and I thank you for letting me ask. Can I suggest what no one else might? Would a caesarean be an acceptable consideration likewise to other choices?

This choice is never or rarely discussed and so then let me reveal the mind of those who might surround you one day. I having no reason to ask, present to you an alternative held secret from the sight within Women's and Human Rights. One that answers a question which we the intuitive always knew there was yet another solution. Maybe this was it.

When...

When the odds are stacked in your favour,

When you have come thus far proving you are
'the better natured'.

Keep rooted in peace.

There continue into the living reality of unity.

Stand your ground 'in peace'

so that you may always have it...

Trust in your strength, of all you have been
given to succeed. You will.

Lift the nation and so too, the world.

(Written from inspiration at the National Wax Museum Plus,
Westmoreland Street, Dublin)

On Greatness

(by being smaller)

Greatness is a path we take up from our own past which is intimately connected to that of our ancestors. If we are blessed, we will know who they are. If we are not then we have to search forward in sacred faith that our creator loved us to bring us into existence and that our journey may be slightly less conventional but with certainty contains more adventure...

~

In truth, we cannot deny all that we were once in the entirety of our history collected, no matter what it is. It all means something, to us.

~

Thus, what we can do is implore God's grace so we revert not to that which once flowed in the blood of our ancestors and resist all temptation of the greed which can easily be inspired to overcome us with such nostalgic drunkenness too.

~

It is in becoming smaller, being less than, we find we can carry more of what is good and right, for us and for others.

Erm, We Have a Problem..

The most constitutional thing to do,

when there is no constitution...

Maybe is to write one...

In business, in pleasure, in politics, in science, in the arts and music...

What is Prayer?

To pray is the greatest act of charity done in the very hope of faith.

(Written at the Blessed Sacrament)

And...

And we are told Christ pursues us! How though our mother calls to us, reaching to us just in time before we dash into some danger. We are blissfully unaware in our naive states.

Never so far we go before we feel that soft jolt of our taken hand. Less others know what such soft touch else they might know that they are well loved.

Holy Spirit, my love, my all in the world. Present yourself to others who know and love their breath as yours.

Holy Spirit, Lover and lead of my whole existence, ever faithful; not so can I say the same. I plead with you, introduce Our Lady of Mercy at your next opportune time and make it so my Brothers first.

Elenor

Beloved Daughter,

The grace of Our Lord Jesus Christ be with you and may you find this note a mention of the reality which may awaken you. Some advice of comfort dearest child.

St Peter. Remember him always in your prayers and never be afraid of Him. He is mighty to his enemies, you are not his enemy. Give him your patience and work within his time. Come to trust him for what he does, I have already prayed you will come to know in time.

St Joseph, be around those models of St Joseph and reject any that are not as he was – chaste and patient.

St Mary Magdalene, remember her too and do not be confused as to the truth. Ask her anything and she will reveal to you what was right and true at the time of her life. Understand her fidelity was imitation reflect...

The church is a family. All families have problems and so, remain as I, impartial, unbiased to anyone of them. See them in the beauty God the Father cast them from and at all times peace, aim at it, walk through it, be it. This takes your sacrifice and has of many others too. You dear daughter, remember this, it was at the command of God the Father you were called into existence, ready for your time, to love and serve the authority as not just I , but thousands have in that glorious name of peace itself – Jesus Christ Jesus.

Pray for me and to me dear child – look for those who exist who are indeed the sons of God and they will show you the way. Child, it is my love and staff I leave you to pick up and bear the light which will bring the fruit of a future neither of us can know, so far ahead as some.

Love the family and love Our Lady of Mercy, who will bless you and yours into eternity in the name of the Father and of the Son and of the Holy Spirit.

'Vene Spiritu Sancti'

Your Spiritual Mother

(who walked this Earth)

Ka Put!

It's important to recognise when something does not work and whether or not you any longer wish to be part of a system or a process which does not produce the fruit that the tongue speaks.

Whether this is a family you were born to, a career, a profession, a relationship or a habit. It's important to recognise when to let it be and let it go its own way. Some people simply take holidays from situations, habits and so on...

You were sent to this world to bring your gift to life and anyone or anything that 'claims' to know you and your gifts may be liars to your face. No one knows the secrets that God gives you, less your gifts. Those who try to doctor your gift are not doctors for there was no need to heal your gift in the first place. You received it in perfect condition. Sobering thought isn't such? How deceived are you already? Sensing something ring true?

Thus, if you are snared in some 'thing' reach into yourself and call forth your glorious soul who will blaze off any remnant gripping and go exactly where you know you should.

If you feel restrained by influences around you, remember this. It's is not you with the delusion of power, it is they. They seek your power, your victimhood, you in a weak and helpless state. See then who the victim is and know who then has the power. They need you to justify their efforts! Simply seek, that they discover humility so that they appreciate what it is to be graced and not consumed by power. Two different things that the world would have you believe are the same. This is the power of self knowledge when you can intimately see the divine reality that you exist in.

For those who know not my Lord Jesus Christ, I pray unceasingly for you in private, say the most potent of prayers and given the grace bestowed on this rather pathetic, worthless sinner (that I am), let me assure you that it is possible with God and God, He knows me and I have just met you. It is He who makes our relationship in these words and this is a way one can also understand prayer too.

Words are powerful and in them a divine relationship. Therefore allow me to intercede for you and say the word, that word I whisper to the Lord so often 'Only say the word and my soul shall be healed'. For you with no rites, let me show you a way, a flicker of truth to bring you home to where we all belong, in the arms and affections of our merciful God. Be merciful therein and know mercy forever more.

On Families

The West is full of broken families. The reason for this is parents who allowed moral deficits or were never taught in morals, or given love which is a most obvious thing to state. Therefore your life has been probably haphazard and affected by their ways. It's a fact and here we remember all those who caught excusitis since the 1960's and so on...

Therefore, refer to good sources and understand this small fact of how you became attached to the world and various co-dependencies of services or relationships...with people, drugs, alcohol, gambling, poverty mindsets, politics (and all the very new ideologies), sexuality and which one (and when), your job, friendships, attitude to health, even pets.

Only you have the right of freewill to govern who and what interacts with your life and where there are markers overstepped in any way stand firm in your understanding that you can move away from or towards any desired outcome you want.

Where something gets in your way find a way of opposing it so that others may know freewill and freedom. It is each and every one of us who can cut the bonds of the past which bound our parents to immoral and unethical practises because they wanted it easier or fell for traps which seemed to make them 'safer' or more 'wealthy'. Accept that the burden is on you and you have the God given power to bring the matter to repent, and it will for you have freewill and freewill is the gift of God absolute.

About families. Remember this 'they did their best' is a way of saying we are sorry at times. It may be too late for you and it might take years of reparation or it may never happen at all. It is as simple as this. As a child you needed love, comfort, support, boundaries, directions and encouragement. Any disruption or abuse will have taken an effect. If you can, forgive and forget. If you must, go no contact because at times families can be passionately dangerous and you can put yourself at risk if you do not fit the profile of their demands. Ultimately, you will be bullied, harassed, coerced and worse if you stay. This is not 'self sacrificing' this is 'self harm'. You know and can predict what will occur but you might be hooked on the absence of care once due. Let me tell you something quietly. You cannot go back in time to get it and they cannot give it you now, no matter what they do. You are likely to see it as phony and it will be. Any action of yours which involves boundaries will be seen as revolting and rebellion (even if you are 55 years old!). This is because you are part of a dynamic life lie or family fantasy at times which in all reality is very fragile. These life lies are intolerable to the growing soul. You suspect sinister working which makes things 'appear' normal. You are right. These things are an apparition to give the world a staged view. That is not the stage of your life story and I would beg you to see this if you are in any kind of relationship/s where this sounds familiar and suddenly you sense there is something in what I am saying here...

Think carefully about boundaries and reach out for support in other social circumstances, engage in them. Once you are free of the mesh, do not go back to it and do not berate yourself for never finding the grounds to trust them again. There is the distinct chance that may never happen.

One thing I can assure you, one day you will find your spiritual family and you will heal, just occasionally we have to experience the mortal life first to know how blessed we are when we arrive home. I hope that you find courage in this because it *can and does* happen. Set out to discover love and you will...

(Written from the inspiration and support from www.womboflight.com a website created by Beth Webster)

Selfishness

"My life is not important to you.

My role in your life is important to you!"

(Interpreted from an interesting conversation sat in Govinda's
Vegan Restaurant, Dublin Centre)

Apathy

(The new sloth)

Apathy of humanitarianism the burnt bridge of the soul in those who feel they have already accomplished enough on behalf of their stewardship.

This of course is nonsense...

'In Truth'

To stand for truth often means being
mistaken for the opposition. Such is
not true. For whose way are you in
and who then is the opposition who
voluntarily stands in front of the
truth of your words..?

and that is all?

Freedom means to not only believe
your truth but to reveal it as truth to
another, if it is truth.

(written at the Wiley Fox, on The Quays, Dublin)

Treasure...

This is the only treasure we have,

we take with us...

Faith

That saves us now and ever...

That stays true to the test of time eternal.

So, what legacy we leave is that we make now
and will look back on with our judge.

Choose the one who loves and forgives you
absolute.

The Problem with Spiritual Abuse

Here is what I humbly conclude from a philosophical and very spiritual view.

'It is the abuse of someone's beliefs by impressing upon them that there is always rational answer to a supernatural response'

Therefore the problem with spiritual abuse is that the protagonist cannot see that 'they are insisting their presupposed beliefs' which consistently represented as 'reliable' or are so 'popularly accepted' so as to be assumed as a 'belief'. They do not feel there is a need to 'substantiate any further proof', assuming it as a type of logic or common place. They cannot perceive the impressing any belief that *they* have entered into the ritual thinking of faith or religion itself which concoct as one, may not have any dogmatic substance or rubrics (rules) that hold accuracy in original understanding or description from its outset. Therefore it is passed on as rationale or reason that is a type of deceit, well formed or not, the intention defines. It is a communication method which spawns from the dysfunction of prudence espousing from the representatives own turmoil dominantly projected. Not to founder a more actual reality but with the ambition of reinforcing their reality, to find comfort in thence inherited objective validations of another.

It is evangelisation of a sort which ignores or refuses to acknowledge the other person's interior peace is equally valid and so aims to disrupt it lodging itself as a type of parasitic thought. This is the prize a constituted proof, an external source of confidence for the affirmation in another's conversion to their belief. Humans desire unity and community. This is one way that person feels no longer lonely and is satisfied that they have created a relationship suitable to be in the worthy company of therein. A natural desire to be gregarious whether it is healthy and humane is something for further meditation.

This results in different behaviours swinging between the radical to the apathetic. Within the once peaceful person, imposturous thinking has been made assertive which requires the effort to undo or live with. It scars for it is a scratch into the core of a person's identity with the intent on conforming them to an idea or a belief; of which they have not themselves been allowed the time to discern against their own spirituality, obligations, cultures or way of life.

Being peaceful means to fully accept and not adapt, adjust, change, manipulate, or ever have the intent to affect in any way during any encounters another's soul; but only to develop the relationship for the sake of good relations which means appreciating fully the others identity in faith, spirituality, limitations and faults, with greater loving tolerance. This means to drop all compulsion to 'teach another a lesson' which in some organisations is a rotted expression of unwanted and uninvited intervention of which is sinister. It is not actually any of their business and closer aligned to bullying and harassment than any posture they may assume in title or rank or power. Teachers, real teachers disclose their aims and objectives to students. Evil doers (even out of stupidity or ignorance) conceal truth and motives. That is how you know what and who you are dealing with. And I remind you, you have a choice to leave politely, quietly and be at peace knowing you at least have the grace to do so.

Any profession that exists now, owing that there is the contract of money involved and policy to mind, means that expressions of be love can be difficult to flourish in human relations. One cannot be sure of the motives of anything contracted aside they will do the job for the money. However, it is not impossible to express our humanity or love in contracts and we should all aim to do so. The Declaration on Human Rights gives us every ground as individuals to take a stand somehow in any such environment, anywhere in the world. We do not realise these secret or hidden treasures and so do not notice. We even might overlook them for we have been flooded by the excessive media folly which has ridiculed them rather tastelessly. We should not allow this to fatigue us in any campaign to uphold human dignities. The difference between a person paid in service to another who acts as in fiduciary is whether or not they will side on the side of protecting another from misuse of powers by the organisation that pays them.

Here is an example; a sergeant major in the 1930's was instructed to punish a man by putting him in a sweat box. He refused and saved the man's suffering for doing so. It is an offence to disobey but he did. These days the world has no need of physical devices for psychological ones can produce the same effects. It is our awareness on what and how we respond to commands or influences which make *right and true, just or fair* that we *should or should not* 'cooperate'. That is all it takes – say no.

Spiritual abuse may be the very start of every abuse for the thought itself is born from a dimension we know not, nor can prove exists. It does not exist until thought of. The grace of having a conscience means we can rationally decide whether or not to continue the thought towards actions or not – that is to STOP IT before it starts as physical action!

For Christians, I urge anyone this. Avail the Sacrament of Reconciliation to help determine the thought you have been given is for good (or not) and there make peace before not only it consumes you and your treasure, but dashes someone else's lives too.

For all faiths, atheists, none believers alike, I urge you to think and reflect on the matter that every religion the world over has its actual feet rooted in the creation of 'peace' itself and it is *for* peace we attempt to define our differences to make such peace. It too is where we get confounded. We disturb the peace by attempting to make peace at times. We accidentally impose our beliefs on the closest and cause spiritual damage, even so where we claim that we have no beliefs. If we can be peaceful there be the prize that allows us all to harmonise an equal opportunity to advance as communities and as individuals.

For all of us, one way we can certainly be at peace with each other is to learn the art of appreciation for observing the unique qualities and benefits others brings into our worlds. It is to learn what the value is in that person and how to navigate ourselves so as to ensure that mutual prosperity is realised. This is done by initially being hospitable and welcoming. Where we cannot be that, at the very least we can be helpful offering examples in acts of faith, hope and charity so that others might see, no matter where or what we are collectively or individually, we still uphold the common care of humanity...

...which is to love tenderly and protect each other.

Four Rules

One Day Every Day Challenge

Rule 1: Have Fun

Rule 2: Make mistakes (we call that learning)

Rule 3: 'Get' from every day

Rule 4: Do better by using Please, Sorry, and Thank You *and...*

Excuse Me...

Choice

"In denying some ones choice we are dictating another's action"

(we can do better than that)

In Heart

What you cannot confess with your tongue, confess with your

heart...

(Written at the feet of Venerable John Sullivan's SJ remains at St Francis Xaviour Church, Gardiner Street Upper, Dublin)

For anyone 18-21 Years Old

Always look like you are going *somewhere* and then face in the *right direction.*

As a child someone always pushed you on the swing and this remains an invisible truth throughout adulthood.

In adulthood we call this friendship, fellowship and fraternity.

Swing!

On Heaven

What 'might' be the experience of Heaven?

"The total security of being alone with Christ so as to know only peace, free from all threat, without a body who's senses limit us; to fully experience the joy and bliss of all we only momentarily glimpse at during Holy Communion"

(Inspired by Francis)

Paternal Love

Paternal love is that love
which   apparent from
the holy attachment in
the *gaze* of a father
reaching for the intimacy
of trust with   children.

(Written after the Tuesday Evening Divine Mercy Mass
at St Saviours, Dublin in 2019)

Sin and Consciousness?

In my humble spiritual understanding I offer these thoughts. It is better to live righteously in this life than take to death a conscience which can accuse you before your maker.

Make peace with everyone and then offer your sacrifice* in life, as dead.

Be right with God and when you succeed in this share with others how.

(*sloth, envy, jealousy, gluttony, hate, lust, deceit, revenge, anger...)

Purgatory

(and a small bit on Hell)

To purge is a way of lancing the parts of a person poisoned and the healing action of reparation, an opportunity to become whole again.

In purgatory if you see a rope which looks like a rosary, take a good hold of it...

Never run in Hell, you may draw attention to yourself...

(and...always ensure you have a rosary and a Crucifix if you visit)

On Crosses

'_We_ are

His Cross'

Modern Day 'Understanding'

*'They' **do not want truth, they want reason to believe what they have come to love is everyone else's** 'truth'...*

(Summarising how an older person feels about any faith in 2019)

God (Jesus) is Our DJ

The mass is possibly the great graphic equalizer of God we can all witness using our freewill. It is in the Holy Sacrifice of the Mass, en mass, we find everyone such from the millionaire to the gangster, the mother to the prostitute, the sandwich maker and the admiral, dignitaries and servants, beggars and thieves, gamblers and bankers, drunks of sin and addicts of mercy, apostles of redemption and virgins so pure of heart of mind, sat right next to the murderer and the innocent. The grieving and the joyous all together in one act of peace amongst each other, allowing God to breathe in and out a single breathe that pours into the world, making true the vision of love, that is God's graces into humanity.

God equalises everyone in the Mass. The sacred mystery made truth at the Elevation of the Host casting His beloved gaze upon us with all intent to ascend once more to Heaven; so that we might be saved from the sins, having sacrificed for our offering, to answer the spoken and unspoken prayers, to cascade healing and mercy due and undue. To refresh and renew our faith inspiring courage and confidence until the sweet end. There face to face we meet our beloved Lord Jesus Christ. Such is to be a fraternity where forgiveness reigns so that hurt can heal and in the world forgiveness can flourish in a society which is unjust.

This is how injustice can be bought to an end; by creating from the dust the clay, which is the beginning of a greater love story than it was at the beginning.

Handover

The most important thing we can do, I so dream, is that we live peacefully in all native lands with each other immigrant, visitor and indigenous alike. It is they, the locals, who indicate the earth's needs and for such experience we can learn how to support our blessed Mother Earth. It is the stranger who thinks they have the right of opinion and a burden of proof which spoils the land with uncomplimentary ideas. Subversive motives of exploitation covered in the mask of good intentions even convince the owner of the latter.

With traditions fraying and our world in need of cultural wisdom and retreat, it is us who lose our peace not they. Peace is already in their hearts, it is ourselves, who need to learn peace and we only do this with those at peace. We achieve this by listening and asking intelligent questions; by submerging ourselves to their culture a while to let it penetrate us.

Respecting lands and protecting culture, not by intrusion and the 'we know best' approach (we do not or there would be peace and prosperity on earth now). It is done by quietly saying sorry and asking how can we help you? Then we can enter into a dialogue where solutions that work for us and the rest of the Earth benefit too.

JOB DONE! (WELL)

THE MERCY OF GOD

GOD IS THAT, HE IS

God is the all that was, is and ever will be. He is the One who, by love of creation, created – for the sake of our joy; for the sake of His Glory. We can add nothing to God but what we are created for is do the same works as He did on earth. This is the vital element in understanding any relationship with God and so being able to receive in accordance with Gods superabundance. As we draw closer to God, so also we draw closer to Gods plan for us. When any one works within the predestined laws of their reality, can they receive in accordance with His will and His plan.

What we receive and how we receive is not our business to question or criticise for we are not God and we do not have the power to shift the universe, so that we might receive - as we would like to. We can but obey God's laws and submit to His will. We can trust in is that what we are given is given for our good. Therefore the precept here is that our judgement is irrelevant – it is our contribution that matters. We are subjects of a merciful God who, by His attribute of generosity, provides uniquely for us. In understanding and embracing this we become Servants of God and show our trust by accepting the position of filial dependence upon Him. That means receiving gratefully anything that we are given.

In doing this we imitate God the Father because, inversely, this is what He is doing for us now and continues to do so with the motive of pure love. He does not question what He gives us so generously and does not ask for anything in return. What is given – is given completely - subject only to the influence of our freewill and that of others free will.

'Freewill: The ability to act independent of outside influence'

Cambridge Dictionary

I note here briefly that this does not separate the concept of 'influence' from human or God. It remains a good basic line of thought.

How and when we are granted or gifted graces and temporal rewards is also in accordance in God's plans for us - individually. We participate in God's plan usually after some absence from God when we find we are lacking in something. Some sort of physical or spiritual reminder that humbles us - opens us to the realisation of the type of creatures we really are - human. This review or examination of conscience, awakens in us the awareness of what more we can achieve in the Glory of God, by partaking in that desired partnership and friendship with God. We abandon oppositional and egocentric mindsets, which overstate our own importance that we make up from within; all that we make ourselves think we are. We cast off ourselves and shed away the menial self-centred connotations. We are faced with a new reality, one that shakes our known reality and shifts our perception, almost by intervention. Often we resist this either induced or self directed introspection. We might disdain it, ignore such an important call and thus it becomes suffering as we denounce the need to correct ourselves. We then fall.

It is when we fall we come to know the mercy of God – for He did not let us perish. Each of us can speak of how we were saved from the worst that was to come, even within limited experience. Who we attribute that to matters but I will continue my mind there later. To round up briefly why we are given some suffering sometimes, it is a jolt to remind us of how blessed we are that God Almighty cared enough to notice such a troublesome creature of His and to intervene. We are interrupted in our discord. The grace filled takes this as providential correction. The self sufficient perceive it as an inconvenience of some kind, an offence against their 'entitlements due to them in life'.

It is these falls with the pains that the shedding of worthless things easily become despised for what they really are; temporary manifestations of self delusion.

GOD IS LOVE & MERCY

God is love and mercy and there is no clearer
description than such. If He were not so, nor would we
be capable of love and mercy; as is the case with all
graces. It is better said we really receive mercy and
interpret that as the love of God. For those who throw
all else aside and take up their cross for the sake of Him,
for the sake of the Fathers Glory, can hold the hope that
our work is good enough to be considered for His
glorification – worthy of such attention. We find
ourselves hoping that we are doing God's Will and God's
Work and this is all we can ask for both in life and death.

For the scientific minded, glorification would look like
magnification, purified, absolute. What we would be
looking at is so blinding it is incomprehensible. It cannot
be subject to a collective description or singly defined
outcome or result. It is not possible to totally observe
God using a single point of examination and neither is it
possible to use all methods of examination to see what
God is. What faculty or tool is there that proves such?
We are in fact denied the means to test God and in this
we find is God's will for us – it is a command spoken
everlasting decreed. We can but be in awe of this
majesty – appreciate it from our single view points and
be grateful so that incrementally it might unfold at His

will. As we are graced with more faculty to receive – the more blessed we become as trusted inheritors and Children of God for such.

What we think or how we may rate something cannot be presented accurately as God sees it. What we see is not what God sees. He sees us completely naked in body and soul. This goes to show His mercy for us. He does not expect such a limited creature to do all that He can, for it is beyond both reason and order. We are not expected to walk perfectly initially and are taught how to walk with God. When we fall, God's mercy comes to our rescue and forms then the foundation which we can stand on.

It is also true we might at this point still not see the benefits or even reject that the Saviour is helping us, carrying us. This is quite simply because we are human and have to retrospectively look back with a sense of appreciation so that it becomes apparent. We cannot appreciate a painting as complete half way through although we might be able to imagine it. Thus, when we are through the testing experiences, it is then we can see so much more of the complete beauty. True forgiveness of our enemies is made possible in this way and so forbearing our suffering is very important as we are shepherded day by day; in our suffering.

WE ARE THAT WE ARE – HUMAN

As humans we edit or emphasise anything according to what we think is best (using our minds), we do so naively attempting to deceive God, others and ourselves of all that we really are or have done.

God all knowingly, knows truth. It's a good thing because very often we don't know what is good for us and we like to be naughty or make believe we know better. Whatever we think, say or do is exposed completely to God and it is on His Mercy we rely. He is omnipotent, omnipresent. Like a child insisting He did not eat the cake, who has chocolate on his lips – the Father knows what we have been doing with our thoughts and deeds, just the same. This is absolutely why we must be familiar with humility. It is God who forgives our grandeur and us who appear foolish to Him for such assumptions that we can hide from Him. It is in humility that we can let God know what we so need to disclose or portray, so that we receive forgiveness and mercy. All that we do forget to mention or lack courage to confront in ourselves, He forgives too. This is how we know we can entrust ourselves to God.

Continuing though with the theme of what God sees. We humans also have an overinflated sense of self and assume we know how to think for ourselves. We still know nothing of where thought comes from and so, in 2017, it is safe to assume we only get to witness the creation of the brain by the actions of thoughts 'thinking'; opposed to the origin of where thoughts first come from or how they are started at conception. Given, that yes thoughts can be stimulated or influenced by using external worldly impressions and experiences, we do continue to learn. However the original thought which came first, that one that arose from our conceptions, remains a glorious mystery. We just know it happens, not where it comes from and yet it is present from our very beginning. Thought is, in my humblest of opinion, from divine inspiration and to be respected for the most awesome of consequences it can have. Nothing made from man (good or evil) ever came about without a human thinking on it first and developing action on that initial thought.

Thinking about thought certainly brings us close to Gods divine nature because here God, being spirit, descends into both mind and heart by the means of means of prayer or mediations, which are ways of thinking on a matter, using methods like Lectio Divina.

Mankind being subject to God, is self motivated as a collective species and so considers (thinks) only those about him and this is what is *only* expected of him. He is commanded to love his neighbour and that means considering his neighbour. He does not have the responsibility of considering all that God does so that the Universe remains obedient. Mankind in itself is graced with this relief and can rely on God for all needs to be addressed thenceforth if he believes so. This is de facto simply because we stand in the providence of Gods activities before, during and after our life. We did nothing of such work and nor are we expected to think on (or consider) such beyond the great command of loving one another. We are well provided for, albeit confused and subjected to by various cultural or economical situations; which are not sent from God. Despite what struggles we face, God remains faithful to us, flowing into the aspects of our lives, which are required to sustain our lives and He does so with love and Mercy.

To make this clearer, for example, God does not simply turn the air off because He is disappointed in our disregard for each other. He is higher in all intelligence and I would humbly say that disappointment is only a human experience. God does not experience disappointment but rather understands that we do and helps us relate our emotions to a more graceful response. Again this comes down to us thinking with God about how we respond to an event; and we need practise at it through prayer, meditations, benediction et al. This is the field we plough so the wheat might grow. The objective being that we imitate the merciful nature of God with each other which propagates love in all mankind. It is through our relationship with God we become able for these higher spiritual challenges. Being internal challenges, this is where we must head first. If we attempt to do this alone, with no mediators or consideration in our relationship with God, we cannot receive the graces necessary that lift us to the higher love, which is sourced only in God's love and mercy.

COGNITO ERGO SUM

"I think, therefore I Am" – Descartes

Thought is where our freewill (shall we do good or shall we do bad?) always comes upon a battery of tests and that is so every second of our lives. We are given the creative license to Co-Create with God imperfectly (because that is what we do and we are not God) by making choices that affect ourselves and others.

We are invited to cooperate with what are perceived as natural scientific laws or those laws of theological virtue. We still have not developed another arm of this framework and so it seems that is all we are ever going to experience. The two schools divided because science demands an isolated identity from theology, whereas theology totally embraces science; although this might not be so well known. In nearly every case of any major scientific discovery ever; the person doing so was faithfully religious. It is no coincidence. However, this conflict that arises from this duality makes us think. Much like a game of ping pong we try to rationalise doubt between the two, and do so until in the face of death if we are in doubt of God's limitless Mercy Divine.

Here I am not simply considering the death of the body but the spiritual death of the soul and those who are ever doubting Gods love and Mercy. By persistently seeking proof of God we miss those opportunities to experience His love and Mercy in the now. In effect we diminish the quality of our own life in the pursuit of the impossible which is actually proven with faith. God, however being Almighty and Mysterious, does not deny us the same way we do Him and indeed remains faithful to us with His Love and Mercy.

In the face of death we always turn to either medicine or faith. True? So then we must consider the Mercy of God who is the original healer and giver of life as the expert Himself. When we face either type of death, the only thing we become interested in is God (or the spiritual) because individually, uniquely God reveals His love by being the Redeemer in that way. We see the effects of His universal power personally. We quickly second the scientific and materialistic because we see the truth in that which enriches our lives – it is revealed to us. We are required to believe in order to acquire the gift of faith. It is no more complex than that. It is the experience of understanding no human can save a soul in the face of death because it is beyond our privilege to know how such is done. These revelations are totally unique and exclusively a private experience.

There are those with near death experiences that offer hundreds of stories about their experience to reveal that actually the science part of life (and all the hassle of superficial material matters) become insignificant. God being merciful knows all this and effortlessly steps in as the Saving Redeemer, with whatever is necessary for each and every one of us, when we face the journey of our lives into death itself. From those I have encountered they assure me that from their experience, they met with only love and mercy. They describe this as peace and bliss too.

We do have a powerful choice in life and that is to acknowledge the awesomeness of God's presence. Swaying in doubt expecting Him to provide yet more miracles, or exhaust ourselves searching in places which are far too young to have qualitative experience, is a costly and unmapped territory of variables. Regardless one must have confidence of being saved with presumption, I hastily add here – He will save everyone who holds faith in Him.

It is important to face truth simply and honestly. We all have proof of God's existence and that is by the fact you are reading this. You are a miracle and should you be in any doubt of that, ask physicist of what the chances of you being born were or what may have happened if the Big Bang occurred only one eighth of a second faster...

...than it did. It was not an accident and nor was the air you breathe or the life you were given as a free gift to experience.

Mind Yourself!

(no one else will)

God is merciful when we realise our error if we cause any harm, ask for forgiveness **and** choose to forgive; so that we might defuse any offences and not return to the same mistake. This is very important to grasp because misuse gives rise to recurring habits. Those habits will bring us not to God but to the one who destroys both body and soul. God, being merciful and the Worlds Redeemer (even in that state) is able easily to preserve our souls should we admit to our uncalled for behaviour. Here, if you feel moved, I would gently prompt you to speak to a priest or religious who will take the upmost interest, giving you some rest and direction to find your peace. I understand what I have said may cause discomfort to the unprepared. That is often a sign of the soul reaching out and communicating with you. The good news is that you heard it again, for the first time or that you are now ready to step to God.

WE ONLY 'THINK' WE ARE SMART

Put simply we do not have the mental or spiritual capacity or faculties to judge how a soul is by using thought; as God can judge by being God. One might say that being love and mercy there is no need for God to think but rather that He acts. He *is* and we often rely on Moses encounter where God explains "I am that, I am". He takes all of His creation into account, owning every part and denying not one part of it.

Spiritually, physically and any kind of 'ally' we attach to the meagre definitions we coin (as a means to communicate to another human description), they cannot be as dynamic or generate such might as that of God's Mercy. He can affect at distance, anything, any time and any place. We have to learn to be satisfied with His Mercy and being forgiveness itself; that in honouring God He will assist us through the Holy Spirit, to bring us to righteousness. This is God's prerogative and in understanding that, we must acknowledge we are lowly and indeed subject to God – the Creator. We have to acknowledge that we receive Mercy and it is our position to reflect love to our neighbour on behalf of God – if we claim we are of Gods Children.

We can only at best estimate, guess or maybe partially predict how our efforts or works are valued by God, but to say we know the sum total of value would be arrogant. The smallest deeds are at times the greatest of Mercies. We will never know the sum of the good (or evil) we do and that is what God can both account for and glorify with His mysterious effects in both our life and death. We are stunningly ignorant.

To assume we can completely value something as God does is just too big to think about. The Saints often reveal this truth – for in all we know about them – we will never know everything about them. There is no computer that can categorise all of the wonders each saint would have done and they still demonstrate. They are an ongoing show of God's providence for us to commune and imitate in the ways they discovered of relating to God. So to keep our minds on why God is merciful, using the Saints in this example; we are merely observers seeing a very small snapshot of all they really were and are now. We can say this of any event or experience – that we are only graced with a pin hole view of any sum total, in any event of anything we do or say ourselves. Gratitude is the fundamental feature for all we have done that we know about and all that we don't know we have done that we are not privileged to know about.

GOD AS THE FATHER OF LOVE & MERCY

God is super intelligent but accepts our best refined ramblings as any Father would his child babbling away in a crib. He makes sense of our needs by our communications. He does not pander to us – He provides for us. Neither father nor baby has any idea what is being said but they are aware that they are in a communion of pure love and mercy. It is a state of intense joy, pleasure, assurance when both sides revel in each other's existence. It is direct and affectionate, full of lessons and loving acts. Each knows His role, one better than the other. This is the order of creation and the seasons of times in lives. They are in what might be described as an authentic relationship. This is the kind of Fatherly love God has for us. However, when God the Father loves us it's on a bigger and more radical scale than when we offer love to Him or as our earth fathers might love us.

Humans love within limitations and whether we accept that as truth and deny our human vulnerability will not make a difference accept to how much more we could have loved. We only let those we love go so far before we find forgiveness incredibly difficult. God is not like that at all because He is an inexhaustible treasury of love and forgiveness. We cannot ever offer the same magnitude of love in return to the Father, but rather it is appreciated in a greater magnitude instead. We do not have any comprehension of this scale and so at best we can simply persist in the practise of loving and forgiving each other to know that we are on the right path.

The greatest example that Christians have of loving the Merciful Father and trusting in His Mercy, is that of Jesus Christ. Christ loves us so much He died for us and submitted His freewill to the will of the Father – who He knew would, in turn, redeem Him by His love in Heaven. This is the pinnacle example of trust we can have in God the Father in Heaven. It is what inspires the same confidence in the most desperate of situation today; that there is hope when we persevere with faith and charity. These are heavy words for the yet learned, but I assure you that the revelation is worth the pursuit of knowing Christ. I would recommend anyone pick up the Gospel of John, being the beloved disciple of Christ, to intuitively gain a great sense of this love and trust I am promoting imitation of.

The Apostles imitated this tradition of love and truth. As we see in the Acts of the Apostles who imitated Christ, in the belief that His witness was the truth; they only knew that they were at the start of something great. This is true of everyone who first glanced Christ and instinctively knew there was more going on than words. There is – a great deal more.

The Apostles were up against all who threatened freedom, but were so inspired by the example of Christ they were able to lay their lives on the foundation of Christ's work. Freedom is what Christ was and is all about. That every human being had his freewill intact and that he might choose to believe of his own will – whatever he so believed. It was a time of enforcement by coercive and clandestine methods so that degrees of the population were controlled and became deaf to their souls.

This leads us to ourselves in the present days – who live on the other side of that time, with our thriving churches and majestic priesthood; who imitate the disciples of Our Lord this day. If Christ was not God's Son, like all passing schools of thought – there would be little proof of His existence now. We have exactly the opposite – more faithful than ever before, the Church, the Bride of Christ continuing to tell the greatest story on earth; so that the Plan of Salvation might be disseminated to those lost and loved sheep of Christ. That sheepfold of God has a home in the church and it is His mercy and love that powers it so they can come out of the weather and be refreshed.

To summarise here briefly, we have no real idea of God's appreciation of ourselves but He has absolute comprehension of what we are and provides for us. Being mercy, he looks down on us with his smiling face and just knows we will never see the same thing in the same way. He simply provides for our needs and that of others without question. We are never going to witness completely everything as God does, despite how we might think we do or excite to think we will. The disciple John realises this ahead of us and offers comfort in his short account which explains that Jesus did far more that is and could be recorded:

"30 Jesus performed many other

signs in the presence of his disciples, which are not recorded in

this
book.[31] But
these are
written that
you may
believe[32]
that Jesus is

the Messiah,
the Son of
God, and
that by
believing
you may...

have life in his name."

John 20:30

We cannot know all that Jesus did but we can see the effects of His most precious life. Thinking on the Rosary the Joyful Mysteries in some detail is certainly helpful if we see even as a child, for example, He created love and affection right from the start. People travelled miles to see Him, greet Him just born into the world. So too, it is true, the moment you have a family you start that experience and personally encounter the invitation to consider by the example of the Holy Spirit, deeper understanding into this insight.

WE ARE NOT ALONE - EVER

Any value we have is insignificant to
the value we are given by the Father
in Heaven. Alas, we realise we are
limited, unprepared for the world
and worse vulnerable to both
temporal and spiritual matters. Faith
in our very lives become a mystery
and teaches us humility from the
outset, thus we are at once saved
from ourselves.

Humans come and go at their will or
better said at the price of sin itself –
death. Our closest spiritual relative
at times, may well be our Holy
Guardian Angel, who depending on
his own position, might be very

clever or super at prayer and adoration (amongst other given graces); so he will be infinitely closer in recognising God than ourselves, helping us return closer to God or performing His given works with grace. Guardian Angels are our unseen helpers and at times, you might have experienced this yourself; something saved you from a very dangerous event, a surprise showed up, you found a lost thing. Often it is your very wise Guardian Angel at work, whether or not you know he is there or believe in him. There are many non-Christian testimonies on Holy Guardian Angels and a quick search on You-Tube lets us know that there is a collective agreement that we are not alone.

God cares so much for us He ordains a Guardian Angel to each of us, as an act of love and mercy. God knows we are ill equipped to deal with the spiritual and He also knows how the spiritual manifests into the temporal. An external counterpart from His Heaven placed on this earth, at our conception, to guide and protect us. That they do and busy they are every moment of our lives.

This reflects our value extraordinarily I find and only a God of Mercy would furnish us with such a privilege. The Guardian Angel is the often disregarded gift that we take little interest in because we are overwhelmed with inaccurate teaching of the spiritual. Guardian Angels are priceless in earthly terms because they can attain for us much grace and gifts from God, which makes present His mercy and grants us the gift of humility itself.

We might complain of God not being merciful enough but fail to realise that it is both humility and gratitude which draws down God's Mercy. It is vital that we are grateful. In terms of angels, we fail to call on (invoke) our Guardian Angels, take them or send them to Mass or Devotion. They like nothing better and it is of my understanding this is very important to them.

Angels are not anywhere near the visual references we might project an angel to be – they are far more powerful and magnificent than simple imagery. They have needs too and work tirelessly to keep us safe day and night. We fail to see with our eyes all the undertakings they perform and so we could be more like God and offer them some consideration. Just because they are mostly unseen and an unproven creative aspect of God – pure spirit; does not mean that we have no responsibility to consider their detainment to ourselves on earth and like God provide them with some refreshment or regard.

God considers every part of His creation and does not pick and choose when any part is distressed. As the healer – He heals. By this word 'heal' I mean reduces or diminishes suffering with the active participation of our freewill. We have to get involved with those processes fully engaging our freewill, so that we receive the healing that we might uniquely need - knowingly and not knowingly. Cooperation and agreement is very important for if we say no – it will be respected. God will wait until we say yes and of course no intervention can occur until we do. God, we might think of in this way, is the perfect gentleman. Catholics imitate this on behalf of others spiritual and temporal needs or difficulties, known as acts of charity, which are motivations from the heart. We offer service, for their benefit whether they are pure spirit, living or deceased. Here we are best to imitate God and remember patience as a virtue, so that we might be recognised as Children of God in that work.

∿∿∿

IF GOD IS MERCIFUL, WHY IS THERE SUFFERING?

It is our neglect of ourselves and others that brings on suffering and God is wrongly accused of allowing suffering. Suffering is not a by-product of God's works and nor is it His intention. It exists as an effect from original sin and as a result our failure to address our self negligence with our intelligence and to restrain our self-centredness. This occurs by being habitualised or conditioned from self deserving cultural influences or we have become complicit with (drawn into) someone else's sin, which originates from Original Sin. It is at all times our participation, approval and cooperation which create any suffering. True those with authority and power can cascade desperate acts of evil because they are ignorant or bought out for thrills and self satisfactions. These are the ones most difficult to avoid and gives us need of examples of both great courage, determination and faith, that in life a heart excited by evil can indeed be pacified to act with better responsibility.

However by using constructively our freewill at any point we can cease ill treating each other and therefore cease suffering around us almost effortlessly. It is wisdom to know this can only be done by each individual cooperating and being knowledgeable on ways to sin and what sin really is. Each individual must make a stand against being corrupted by putting self interests above the needs of his neighbour and profiting (or coveting) from sin. It is means only to the route of evils and death.

It is our self consuming nature which does not reflect God's Mercy, which we can imitate with practise at a human level and which if imitated would bring about greater joys in all our existence. Easy said and I appreciate this might give rise to a defensive response in some people. To those I would say that your faith is being honed and you are called on all the more. Your awareness makes this apparent. You will know there is more to what I am saying and desire to question and even challenge why we should sacrifice something we want to feel good about so that our neighbour feels good instead. Thus hold true to your faith and look further into those feelings – dig very deep and be very honest with yourself. It is often the case things start to improve once one understands ones involvement and makes tracks away from such actually undignified behaviour. We start to experience a fully sense of life.

Love Hurts

Often too, mankind does not appreciate suffering as being the very grounding of all Gods works or intervention. This is who He came to serve and save. The virtuous are prepared all the more to serve his neighbour and so are already comforted. There is little need for the Lords intervention and rather the emphasis is on them to deliver the Lords Services instead. They will know already how to work with God in mind, give rightful praise and have a definite solidity about their personage.

Regardless and in all cases it is not hard to know joy from suffering and it is not difficult to induce suffering on those we say we love. It is simply done by not maintaining relationships in accordance with their purpose. We describe this as damaging our relationship with God. This is because it is offensive to God's Creation and we will find consequences to our behaviours and thoughts, if gone too far will cause suffering emotionally, spiritually or physically. Being creative you will know what I mean here in this example. Let's say that you just finished building a beautiful matchstick aeroplane toy or sand castle. It's a gift for someone you love. Another walks in and smashes it up. You are offended because what you built was unique, right? You cannot do that again in the same way etcetera. Now, God really loves His creation and when he see's us cause harm to each other we quickly find that we are cast off from Him and without His protection.

Jesus has the mystical ability to judge the living and the dead and remains obedient. This is why we should have a natural and healthy fear of the Holy Spirit for it is He who will offer up all that we are so that we might be saved. The Holy Spirit is omnipresent. We can only go so far before we find the rod or staff before us. This is a gift of, to and for the faithful, often not discussed so openly because it is both real and immeasurable in all His dynamics. It is a natural Holy Fear but more similar to respecting the nature of water than not daring to live fully. We know there are rules to swimming safely and so can work well within them and our limitations. The biggest limitation at all time being that we never take position as God in any way and this is considered carefully because it is so easily intrigued by temptation.

It is imperative to truly receive Gods love and mercy; we act in accordance with our purpose and embrace our experiences with deep gratitude. Here I propose that we are also to care for, according to their purpose in life, the people and things we are given, so as not to offend God or our neighbour – who like in God by his/her soul is made in the image and likeness of God. We can all ask both our neighbour and God for forgiveness. That is a beautiful gift. Corals do not do that when they have eaten their neighbour to gain more space and grow bigger on a reef. We can co-exist by rational communication.

God being merciful offers us providence, asks that we love our neighbour and do our bit of given work towards His plan. If you are man or woman of God, this should be aligned with God's will, your purpose and ones work becomes easy to define. If you are a lay person, it is the religious who can bring about the gentle awakenings necessary so that you appreciate any suffering and revel in the joys of life equally. You might experience co-inherence whereby your load is eased simply by encounters as you witness the more mysterious aspects in the Body of Christ – the Church.

To receive Gods love and mercy, in short, we are to use all things as they were intended by the creator. God remains merciful and does not change – granting us the hope that we might make good of what we have violated of His Creation. He forgives us for spoiling that which we have no right to. He grants situational forgiveness from our neighbours, helping make good our errors and glorifying all that He can, overcoming any circumstance when we return back to the right path.

He forgets we ever offended Him and converts all suffering to love – in death or in our mortal lives. That is mercy in itself. This is what we are expected to imitate or practise to the maximum of our own potential and are granted this wisdom so we might be like the Father:

35But love your enemies, do good to them, and lend to them, expecting nothing in return. Then your reward will be great, and you will be sons of the Most High; for He is kind to the ungrateful and wicked. 36Bemerciful, just as your Father is merciful.37Do not judge, and you will not be judged. Do not condemn, and you will not be condemned. Forgive, and you will be forgiven....

Matthew 6:36

When God is perceived to be not merciful, it is very often because we have forgone the Golden Rule found in Matthew 7:12 and often referred to as (for the taste of the masses) the Law of Reciprocity. In scripture it states:

"Therefore whatever you desire for men to do to you, you shall also do to them; for this is the law and the prophets."

This only shows our dumbest ignorance when we become so complacent we do not take care to remember the simplest of rules. God's power can equally overcome this because He has authority, dominion and the Heavenly powers which afford Him the greater flexibility in responding to our needs; when we supplicate ourselves in a state of contrition. Even though we might have offended grievously our neighbour, for Catholics, we have the Mass and the Confiteor (for pardon and petition) we pray during the Mass, we also have the Sacrament of Reconciliation in its dignified expression. Sometimes the Confiteor is referred to as the Mea Culpa (Latin: through my fault).

IF YOU DRINK TOO MUCH WINE, YOU WILL GET A HANGOVER, POSSIBLY MUGGED OR WORSE...

We humans get drunk very easily with emotion and desires. This is because exercising our freewill is the drug of choice for all mankind living and past. Enjoyment though can carry us straight into addictions and here we find the myriad of traps and snares – simply by forsaking our self control.

When we abuse our freewill, all that we are given and abuse so in discord; we will destroy ourselves and our freewill eventually. This might take generations, but it does happen, for example Sodom and Gomorrah. God does not interfere or stop us in our actions because He would be interfering with our freewill and being Merciful, He has to let that happen. God does not break His word when He gives us something and freewill is what we are given as a gift. Whether we use it responsibly is the turning point in each life story. True?

Humans were given freewill in the Garden of Eden and like the angels, we never had that retained or detained from ourselves. It is part of being human and woe betides anyone who takes the mind to interfere with any human's freewill – it is a gift from God so interference tends to cause some bother for those who interfere with it – in life or death. The consequences deprive us of Salvation. Despite how we use or abuse our freewill it is the same way home for those contrite of heart. So then it is truly available to those also who most grievously offend. No one is beyond God's mercy. No matter how we turn from God he doesn't turn from us. He, being merciful, considers us all valuable and all repairable and remains constantly available to us.

We are both graced and spoiled with freewill at times and easily become complacent or over confident – presuming in God's mercy, weighing up our own merits as valuable in themselves. This is not wise. In acting this way we actually lie to ourselves and deny the goodness of God – we assume what we want comes by our will alone. We have become accustomed to being 'in control'. It is a lie; we do not have any control aside the grace of self-control. In that state of delusion we find something known as self glorification and it is deceit too; because it might flatter the maximum of human potential, but the very least of God's efforts. Therefore, in such thinking and believing we deprive ourselves of all the good we could bear witness to.

If we instead entrusted and included God in any consideration to do with our freewill we would stand aside the greatest advocates known ever in the World.

God see's all this complacency and when we turn back to Him, He still mercifully loves us seeing our contrition of heart, our pains, losses and hurt; if we have come to realise the truth of our nature.

Can we be Merciful to God?

No. God is greater that the collective total of love in all mankind that was, that is and that is to come. Furthermore, God is not human and so we perceive Gods Love as Mercy – that is those unique mystical actions which are given to us, uniquely for our good. Anything that is not good and does not do us good, is not from God. Men who have unearthed that destructive nature of evil and propagated that in the heart of his neighbour are not Children of God. People who imitate their example are also not Fathered from God. They can given the inclination, be saved by Jesus and adopted by the Heavenly Father. So there is hope and most of us would have been subject to agents and allies of destructive forces so we know what we are dealing with – and have a choice not to.

God is greater than the sum of us and the world in which we live. He acts in the silence so helping the little ones to achieve the maximum of their potential through His grace and from no other place can we be more like to God than in our souls. There we find Him first and also at our last. We cannot in effect be merciful to the one who perpetually gives us life or to Him that breathes life within us. This is He who no other intelligence can say brings something out of nothing, to absolute creative perfection, from the motive of pure love, to love and to be able to receive His love, thus becoming an object of love itself.

We cannot trade or give anything to God either. He can create anything. He has no need of us. We are so far removed from how God loves us that we fail to see our existence is because of Him alone. We also, because of blinding manipulation in our lives and social demands or expectations, fail to see this relationship is the way and is the invitation to Eternal Life. We live through the same unique original love, of Father for the son that we too can return to Him, God the Father. It is my opinion that our existence is an act of God's love in itself and for no other reason.

What we can do by appreciation of this mystery is *'take and make'* in accordance to God's will and plan. In doing so we are endowed with all that is necessary to carry out that plan which we have become familiar with. Heading towards God's plan is equally as valid as knowing one is on that same plan. It is the direction we look that brings us to that divine destination in life and death. We only need to look the right way and follow our good hearts.

Occasionally we become unstuck, when awestruck, on how much God has done for us. This is true of my experience. It certainly had a profound effect when I was graced with a sweeping glance over all the providence which had done so much for my sanctification. I never saw it in direct action at the time. It was only in sincere retroactive reflection I was overwhelmed with the amount of universal effort my salvation took. I was breath taken by how little effort I had made compared to that of God's merciful interventions. I suddenly felt indebted; truly I was and remain so.

What else then can we do with respect to repaying God? Primarily accepting we cannot repay a bean is comforting and too can bring about some humanistic type of worry. What we can do is give rightful praise and thanks as a very small (but extraordinarily valued) human expression of gratitude to God. We can remain liberated and be faithful to the 10 Commandments and the command of Jesus "Love one another as I have loved you". As we are put to the test by less experienced people on that spiritual path, we can look to Jesus' examples from the Gospels and seek comfort there. That is all we have to do to be happy.

I would suggest that we remember the smallest act is of the greatest service to God. The moving of a wilting sunflower into the light, the appreciation of the natural wonders, the seeing out of a beloved family member, the praying for the enemies and asking they be graced to know the Fathers love intimately. We also can be charitable, hold unfailing hope and faith in the unseen.

If you feel particularly awestruck, I would seek a spiritual director who can take you further into that love story between you and the Holy Trinity; for you will only benefit in learning the ways of rightful worship and come to know your faith (yourself) as the gift that you know it to be already. It runs deep and far. Interpreting it all is a wondrous and private journey.

TO CONCLUDE

God lets us choose to or not to do anything and everything. He is the great free lover of man. He allows us to turn toward or against Himself – remaining there regardless of what we do. This is a merciful God. There is no escape from God because He is the only constant in the universe and ever present. Yet as many prophetic conclusions draw, if we align ourselves with God's will, we will be provided for and accompanied in our journey, because we are with him or inviting Him – depending on how developed we are in our sense of faith. The prophets also conclude that we cannot accomplish the journey alone and we need always to be searching for the traces of the Divine in our lives; each step being glorified with God's blessing, as we draw closer to His plan for ourselves. We find ourselves on an actual journey of faith *in life,* because of the effects of our own freewill. No matter what we want or do; God reveals what is best for us, leaving us to welcome Him further.

Catholics and Christians are instructed very simply in mercy itself. We are expected to be merciful and equally as forgiving as God the Father and Jesus Christ, as we see in Matthew 6. We can imitate the Father, for this is how we come to know God as the Son, who became human so that we might know the Father. We imitate them both as a great providential privilege, of well founded knowledge from our human history that graciously learnt about God, so that we might too. Many people in the Bible and the forgotten faithful never had the wisdom we do now two thousand years later. We are graced to hold such wisdom and should make haste to acquire the parts we are graced to be filled with.

If we want to experience God then too, we must trust in the temporal and supernatural guidance, so that we can be as God would want us to be – living in everything in the fullness of His light, to the maximum richness of every life event – as His Child. In this way we can come close to seeing what God sees of ourselves. We can only do so by inviting Him to show us such. We must remember that we are to be obedient to the Will of the Father, so that we imitate the Son and are therefore recognised in terms of love and mercy of the same Father, who sent Our Lord Jesus Christ so that we might be saved.

As a closing remembrance in the words here and to glorify God for all that He is to so many faithful. God is love and mercy – therefore so should we be, no matter how difficult the task that is set before us. If we want true communion with God then first we must bow in humility to our Creator and ask Him to bring us to our rightful spiritual home; so that we might learn what it is to be a Child of God in this lifetime. He wants you to live a full life and raise you up no matter where you are at, whatever fault you hold in yourself or however you might have sinned – really...

He loves you so;
He will reveal
Himself to you
personally.

Let Him...

Morality and the Law of the Lands

Just because it's not illegal does not make it immoral;

thus just because it's legal does not mean it is immoral...

What will happen if you don't do that? Is the most potent question you will ever ask yourself to define the loss of you gains unspoken...

God's Speed, God bless and God's peace be with you ever and always in humility and understanding of others.

Why Is The Declaration of Human Rights In Here?

Most people have never have the opportunity to read or respond to the declaration but have some awareness it exists. Unless you know the rights no one can be sure they are taking part in them or defend themselves using them.

To create the opportunity to become familiar and advance the cause of peace in every place we can they are included here.

It is only by engaging with the material can we be actors ourselves in the places it matters for it has and always has been true it is people who have the power and it is the master who needs the servant. Therefore too, it is an example of serving like Christ.

It is when we use our rights we have them and when we uphold them for others can we advance peace and prosperity in some of the most unlikely dialogue which goes unnoticed. Verily I tell you, peace disturbs nothing yet holds everything together in creative harmony. That is why we should keep it.

Universal Declaration of Human Rights

As provided by the United Nations

Preamble

Whereas recognition of the inherent dignity and of the equal and inalienable rights of all members of the human family is the foundation of freedom, justice and peace in the world,

Whereas disregard and contempt for human rights have resulted in barbarous acts which have outraged the conscience of mankind, and the advent of a world in which human beings shall enjoy freedom of speech and belief and freedom from fear and want has been proclaimed as the highest aspiration of the common people,

Whereas it is essential, if man is not to be compelled to have recourse, as a last resort, to rebellion against tyranny and oppression, that human rights should be protected by the rule of law,

Whereas it is essential to promote the development of friendly relations between nations,

Whereas the peoples of the United Nations have in the Charter reaffirmed their faith in fundamental human rights, in the dignity and worth of the human person and in the equal rights of men and women and have determined to promote social progress and better standards of life in larger freedom,

Whereas Member States have pledged themselves to achieve, in co-operation with the United Nations, the promotion of universal respect for and observance of human rights and fundamental freedoms,

Whereas a common understanding of these rights and freedoms is of the greatest importance for the full realization of this pledge,

Now, Therefore THE GENERAL ASSEMBLY proclaims THIS UNIVERSAL DECLARATION OF HUMAN RIGHTS as a common standard of achievement for all peoples and all nations, to the end that every individual and every organ of society, keeping this Declaration constantly in mind, shall strive by teaching and education to promote respect for these rights and freedoms and by progressive measures, national and international, to secure their universal and effective recognition and observance, both among the peoples of Member States themselves and among the peoples of territories under their jurisdiction.

Article 1.

All human beings are born free and equal in dignity and rights. They are endowed with reason and conscience and should act towards one another in a spirit of brotherhood.

Article 2.

Everyone is entitled to all the rights and freedoms set forth in this Declaration, without distinction of any kind, such as race, colour, sex, language, religion, political or other opinion, national or social origin, property, birth or other status. Furthermore, no distinction shall be made on the basis of the political, jurisdictional or international status of the country or territory to which a person belongs, whether it be independent, trust, non-self-governing or under any other limitation of sovereignty.

Article 3.

Everyone has the right to life, liberty and security of person.

Article 4.

No one shall be held in slavery or servitude; slavery and the slave trade shall be prohibited in all their forms.

Article 5.

No one shall be subjected to torture or to cruel, inhuman or degrading treatment or punishment.

Article 6.

Everyone has the right to recognition everywhere as a person before the law.

Article 7.

All are equal before the law and are entitled without any discrimination to equal protection of the law. All are entitled to equal protection against any discrimination in violation of this Declaration and against any incitement to such discrimination.

Article 8.

Everyone has the right to an effective remedy by the competent national tribunals for acts violating the fundamental rights granted him by the constitution or by law.

Article 9.

No one shall be subjected to arbitrary arrest, detention or exile.

Article 10.

Everyone is entitled in full equality to a fair and public hearing by an independent and impartial tribunal, in the determination of his rights and obligations and of any criminal charge against him.

Article 11.

(1) Everyone charged with a penal offence has the right to be presumed innocent until proved guilty according to law in a public trial at which he has had all the guarantees necessary for his defence.

(2) No one shall be held guilty of any penal offence on account of any act or omission which did not

constitute a penal offence, under national or international law, at the time when it was committed. Nor shall a heavier penalty be imposed than the one that was applicable at the time the penal offence was committed.

Article 12.

No one shall be subjected to arbitrary interference with his privacy, family, home or correspondence, nor to attacks upon his honour and reputation. Everyone has the right to the protection of the law against such interference or attacks.

Article 13.

(1) Everyone has the right to freedom of movement and residence within the borders of each state.

(2) Everyone has the right to leave any country, including his own, and to return to his country.

Article 14.

(1) Everyone has the right to seek and to enjoy in other countries asylum from persecution.
(2) This right may not be invoked in the case of prosecutions genuinely arising from non-political crimes or from acts contrary to the purposes and principles of the United Nations.

Article 15.

(1) Everyone has the right to a nationality.
    (2) No one shall be arbitrarily deprived of his nationality nor denied the right to change his nationality.

Article 16.

(1) Men and women of full age, without any limitation due to race, nationality or religion, have the right to marry and to found a family. They are entitled to equal rights as to marriage, during marriage and at its dissolution.
(2) Marriage shall be entered into only with the free and full consent of the intending spouses.
(3) The family is the natural and fundamental group unit of society and is entitled to protection by society and the State.

Article 17.

(1) Everyone has the right to own property alone as well as in association with others.

(2) No one shall be arbitrarily deprived of his property.

Article 18.

Everyone has the right to freedom of thought, conscience and religion; this right includes freedom to change his religion or belief, and freedom, either alone or in community with others and in public or private, to manifest his religion or belief in teaching, practice, worship and observance.

Article 19.

Everyone has the right to freedom of opinion and expression; this right includes freedom to *hold opinions without interference* and to seek, receive and impart information and ideas through any media and regardless of frontiers.

Article 20.

(1) Everyone has the right to freedom of peaceful assembly and association.

(2) No one may be compelled to belong to an association.

Article 21.

(1) Everyone has the right to take part in the government of his country, directly or through freely chosen representatives.
(2) Everyone has the right of equal access to public service in his country.
(3) The will of the people shall be the basis of the authority of government; this will shall be expressed in periodic and genuine elections which shall be by universal and equal suffrage and shall be held by secret vote or by equivalent free voting procedures.

Article 22.

Everyone, as a member of society, has the right to social security and is entitled to realization, through national effort and international co-operation and in accordance with the organization and resources of each State, of the economic, social and cultural rights indispensable for his dignity and the free development of his personality.

Article 23.

(1) Everyone has the right to work, to free choice of employment, to just and favourable conditions of work and to protection against unemployment.
(2) Everyone, without any discrimination, has the right to equal pay for equal work.
(3) Everyone who works has the right to just and favourable remuneration ensuring for himself and his family an existence worthy of human dignity, and supplemented, if necessary, by other means of social protection.
(4) Everyone has the right to form and to join trade unions for the protection of his interests.

Article 24.

Everyone has the right to rest and leisure, including reasonable limitation of working hours and periodic holidays with pay.

Article 25.

(1) Everyone has the right to a standard of living adequate for the health and well-being of himself and of his family, including food, clothing, housing and medical care and necessary social services, and the right to security in the event of unemployment, sickness, disability, widowhood, old age or other lack of livelihood in circumstances beyond his control.
(2) Motherhood and childhood are entitled to special care and assistance. All children, whether born in or out of wedlock, shall enjoy the same social protection.

Article 26.

(1) Everyone has the right to education. Education shall be free, at least in the elementary and fundamental stages. Elementary education shall be compulsory. Technical and professional education shall be made generally available and higher education shall be equally accessible to all on the basis of merit.
(2) Education shall be directed to the full development of the human personality and to the strengthening of respect for human rights and fundamental freedoms.

It shall promote understanding, tolerance and friendship among all nations, racial or religious groups, and shall further the activities of the United Nations for the maintenance of peace.
(3) Parents have a prior right to choose the kind of education that shall be given to their children.

Article 27.

(1) Everyone has the right freely to participate in the cultural life of the community, to enjoy the arts and to share in scientific advancement and its benefits.
(2) Everyone has the right to the protection of the moral and material interests resulting from any scientific, literary or artistic production of which he is the author.

Article 28.

Everyone is entitled to a social and international order in which the rights and freedoms set forth in this Declaration can be fully realized.

Article 29.

(1) Everyone has duties to the community in which alone the free and full development of his personality is possible.

(2) In the exercise of his rights and freedoms, everyone shall be subject only to such limitations as are determined by law solely for the purpose of securing due recognition and respect for the rights and freedoms of others and of meeting the just requirements of morality, public order and the general welfare in a democratic society.

(3) These rights and freedoms may in no case be exercised contrary to the purposes and principles of the United Nations.

Article 30.

Nothing in this Declaration may be interpreted as implying for any State, group or person any right to engage in any activity or to perform any act aimed at the destruction of any of the rights and freedoms set forth herein.

Agreement to Participation with the

Declaration of Human Rights Act 1948

I (Name)_____ agree to uphold at all
times or work towards, where I fall short of any standard set
within the Declaration of Human Rights 1948 signed in Paris,
France on the 10th December in 1948.

I fully commit myself in the same spirit as the original drafters
Dr.Charles Malik (Lebanon), Alexandre Bogomolov (USSR),
Dr. Peng-chun Chang (China), René Cassin (France), Eleanor
Roosevelt (US), Charles Dukes (United Kingdom), William
Hodgson (Australia), Hernan Santa Cruz (Chile), John P. Humphrey
(Canada), to herein act in the full confidence and belief that it is
possible to advance all human intelligence and achievement by
engaging in practise which support each of these articles in words
and deeds.

In all the environments and duties I fulfil, and when in doubt of
any action, I commit to consider the weight of these points of the
said articles and move towards my own self growth providing and
furnishing the world a living example worthy of considering as
exemplary as it can be for that time and place. With that in mind
and to draw upon the people who have most inspired me in
supporting my rights whether known professionally or in the
spotlight of fame and those are called:

_____

_____

_____

_____

_____

209

_____

_____

_____

_____

_____

_____

_____

_____

_____

_____

_____

_____

_____

It is with these people I choose to stand shoulder to shoulder in solidarity with to overcome the contagious malevolence that the world faces and as such I align myself to participate in the good that the world can bring as one race, that we call the human race.

This I sign in the presence of a likeminded person who truly understands what it is to be human and overcome the difficulties we face today that shall and will be dispersed by tomorrow.

Signed by_____ (yourself)

Signed by _____ (Witness)

Dated _____ of_____ this Year_____

Commended Organisations Notable of Mention

This is a small respectable list of recommended and reliable organisations who can be contacted for information and support in respect of their particular responsibilities who are trusted in counsel, prayer, advice and guidance across fields spanning ecumenism, dialogue, education, relations, charity, religious life, publications, media and volunteering.

Pax Christi International – International Catholic Peace Movement (est. 1945 and works in all areas of peace; human rights, economic justice, conflict prevention, peace building and reconciliation, interfaith dialogue, peace education, and ecology and peace holding a consultative status with the UN and the Council of Europe)

United Nations Commissioner of Human Rights – as per countries commissioner

Aid to the Church in Need (ACN) – resources, publications.

Congregation of the Blessed Sacrament (SSS) Eucharistic Adoration and Charismatic Prayer (Scotland and Eire)

St Josephs Young Priest Society, Dublin (Eire)

Gods Cottage, House of Prayer – Glendalough (Eire)

Secular Institute (of Pontifical Right), Dublin (Eire)

Totus Tuus Magazine, (Eire)

SVP (St Vincent De Paul) Charity – receives and distributes donations worldwide. (International)

212

The Ecumenical Society of the Blessed Virgin Mary (ESBVM) – UK

London Interfaith Centre – Venue and Education (UK)

Caritas India – the relief and development arm of the Catholic Church (India)

The Salvation Army (International Aid, advice, support)

Knights of Columbus (International Men's Organisation of Charity)

Chapel of the Lady of All Nations, Amsterdam (Holland)

Lyric FM – who provide very diverse music ideal for study and writing (Eire)

RTE – The Irish National Broadcaster and home of Irish entertainment for TV and visual production (Eire)

Classic Hits FM – Ireland's most renowned radio show with more awards than one can count. (Eire)

The Parnell, Dublin - A historic bar/restraint which has been an inspiration to my writing endlessly. (Eire)

The RTE and BBC symphony orchestras - who have accompanied my works on many occasions. (Eire and UK)

The National Concert Hall, Dublin – which goes without saying is a feature of Dublin History well worth seeing any event at. (Eire)

The Statue of Liberty in New York

Times Square and Ground Zero (New York)

British Broadcasting Corporation (London, England)

National Wax Museum Plus, Westmoreland Street, Dublin (Eire)

Madam Tussauds, London, England and New York, USA

LBC Radio, England (Eire)

Capital 1 Radio, (England)

The British Museum, London, (England)

The New York Times (USA)

Sky Broadcasting, Worldwide

Virgin (USA)

Washington Post (USA)

Bankok Post (Asia)

CNN, CNBC (USA)

ITV, Channel 4 Broadcasters (UK)

The Mirror, Mail, Sun, Financial Times, Herald and so many more daily newspapers in the UK.

And...

Every service member and personnel member in civil and state service who makes it happen for the richest people on earth those of us who are served by them.

How we miss that point....

See...

VIP Notes

These are my very important notes about anything
that comes to mind or moves my heart...

VIP Notes

VIP Notes

VIP Notes

VIP Notes

VIP Notes

VIP Notes

VIP Notes

About the IPCC

The International Peace Collective Collaboration is a group of individuals who may or may not know each other; who write and work under various pseudonyms in order to deliver various stories and texts to the world so that peace might be ever more apparent in the day to day realm we call life.

These are people who want to present works without prejudice of what you already know about them. Often when anyone picks up a book it is their prejudice which spoils the meaning or the message. The message is literally lost in translation. The IPPC aims to be obviously, obviously not; so that you might see the obvious in the presentation of the words.

'They' are:

An international intellectual platform of people who produce works of interest and 'They' form the:

International Peace Collective Collaboration

A community of people who choose to write under pseudonyms leaving you to enjoy the work without the influence of anything other than the effort they have made on your life.

Produced under the auspices of Four Real Publishers, it is as the light should be...

It touches you and you can't touch it...

In the event you feel that you have a copy of something worth presenting to the world without prejudice of yourself then we will be in contact by the usual means or you will contact us by the usual means.

We thank you and hope that you will find all of our writers works herein valuable and purposeful in accordance to their character and personality which is most efficacious and veracious in vertatis, intellectual and emotional, industrious and ergonomic (neuropathically speaking), fun and fictional, relevant and reliable, tasteful and taming, inspiring and edifying.

Above all it is above you so that you might reach for a part you may never thought you would catch in your bucket. A star that fell from the sky for you...

''BIG DOG...

WE ARE HISTORY...''

www.ingramcontent.com/pod-product-compliance
Lightning Source LLC
Chambersburg PA
CBHW071401160426
42812CB00085B/1014